D0646844

1.00.

modern top-down knitting

Sweaters, Dresses, Skirts & Accessories
Inspired by the Techniques of Barbara Walker

KRISTINA McGOWAN

PHOTOGRAPHS BY GUDRUN GEORGES

STC CRAFT | A MELANIE FALICK BOOK   NEW YORK

For Margit

Published in 2010 by Stewart, Tabori & Chang
An imprint of ABRAMS

Text copyright © 2010 by Kristina McGowan
Photographs copyright © 2010 by Gudrun Georges

Library of Congress Cataloging-in-Publication Data:
McGowan, Kristina.
Modern top-down knitting / Kristina McGowan ; photography by Gudrun Georges.
     p. cm.
Includes bibliographical references and index.
ISBN 978-1-58479-861-3 (alk. paper)
1. Knitting—Patterns. I. Title.
TT825.M3857 2010
746.43'2—dc22
                              2010003325

Editor: Liana Allday
Designer: Anna Christian
Production Manager: Tina Cameron

The text of this book was composed in Tribute and Neutraface.

Printed and bound in Hong Kong

10 9 8 7 6 5 4 3 2 1

Stewart, Tabori & Chang books are available at special discounts when purchased in quantity for premiums and promotions as well as fundraising or educational use. Special editions can also be created to specification. For details, contact specialsales@abramsbooks.com or the address below.

ABRAMS
THE ART OF BOOKS SINCE 1949
115 West 18th Street
New York, NY 10011
www.abramsbooks.com

contents

introduction

A copy of Barbara Walker's book *Knitting from the Top* sat on my shelf for several years before I actually had the patience to read it and begin to understand what a gem it is. An avid knitter, I was well aware of the innovative books by both Walker and Elizabeth Zimmermann—prolific and groundbreaking authors whose published works from the mid-1950s to early 1980s changed the face of American knitting altogether. But whenever I would flip through the first few pages of Walker's book, specifically, I always felt that I didn't yet have the skills required to understand or execute her techniques. The prospect of designing my own sweaters was daunting, and I always wound up putting the book back on my shelf, thinking, "Maybe someday I'll figure all of this out."

When I landed a job managing and teaching classes at a knitting store in Manhattan's SoHo neighborhood in the fall of 2004, I considered it a welcome opportunity to finally learn all I could about yarn and construction techniques and design. Part of my homework, I decided, would be to revisit Walker's book. And when I finally gave it a chance, I quickly discovered that not only were no elaborate skills required, but the ideas were exciting and revelatory, forcing me to reconsider everything I thought I knew about garment construction. I was instantly intrigued by the questions Walker posed: Why create a bunch of pieces only to have to sew them together afterwards? Why not create an item as one continuous piece and save yourself a mountain of finishing? And why not start at the top and be able to slip the item on over your head at any stage and adjust the length and fit accordingly? The overall message was an empowering one: measure yourself, dive in, look at your work, think as you go, and take control of your knitting. All of this was new to me and made great sense.

Walker's instructions and diagrams were often a challenge for me to follow. So I set aside time each morning before work to have a cup of coffee and read through a section of the book, carefully taking notes as I went along. Her wit and enthusiastic writing charmed me. "This is delightful and mysterious," she wrote of set-in sleeves, "and makes you feel like some manner of miracle worker." Or, at the end of a particularly involved set of instructions for her sleeveless sweater template: "Now

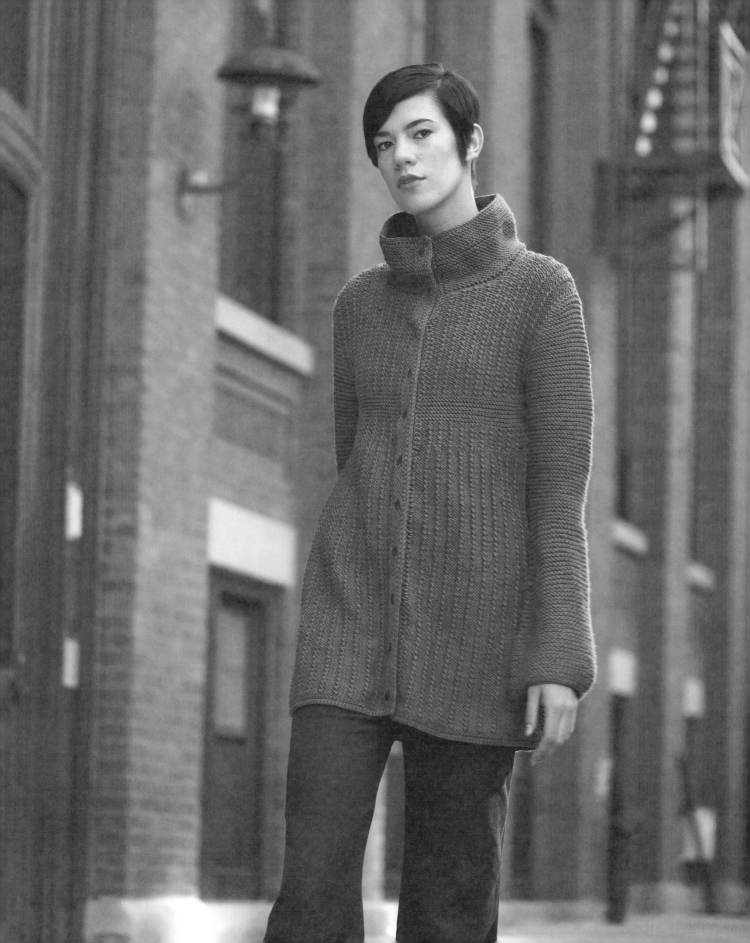

see what a wonder you have wrought . . . don't you feel clever?" Executing Walker's ideas did make me feel clever—clever and inspired—and learning the steps involved to create a piece from the top down seemed nothing short of magical to me.

The more I read, the more I learned, and eventually I completed my first top-down piece, which was the Pavement Jacket (presented on the previous page). I was so pleased with how it turned out that I wrote a letter to Walker to express my admiration of her book and ideas. I did not expect to receive a response and was delighted when, just a few days later, my postman handed me a small envelope with "B. Walker" neatly typed in the upper corner. "No way!" I muttered to myself as I walked to the park to open it. A few weeks and a few letters later, I was in Nokomis, Florida, sitting at Walker's kitchen table, drinking Country Time lemonade and flipping through a stack of albums of fully knitted outfits (including sweaters with matching skirts, dresses, and pants suits) she had created in the 1970s. I marveled at the joy and pride she exhibited in wearing all of these pieces, and smiled at the poses she struck while wearing dark, mod sunglasses.

Her humble and dismissive reactions to my unrestrained gushing were not unexpected. At 79, her bright, kind eyes always seemed to be asking, "What's the big deal?" Still I couldn't help thinking how unfair it was to be the only one seeing these pieces and wishing I had more than just one day to carefully go through each item and ask questions. In a spare room, she unpacked a cedar chest and took out some of the most beautiful knitted blankets I'd ever seen, including a glorious fuchsia throw that mimicked a flower with petals cascading from the center. We also discussed one of my favorite stitch patterns—the Spider Panel from the third volume in her *Treasury of Knitting Patterns* series. "I was simply curious about twist stitches," she explained, "and wanted to give the spider idea a try." As she told me this, I felt a great sense of hope and possibility, wondering what other creations were possible if I was curious enough to try. "There's always a way," Walker said of executing a construction idea. "And figuring it out is the fun part."

In the weeks that followed my return to New York, I sketched ideas in a notebook and mined Walker's book for ideas. For most of the sweaters and dresses, I used her top-down set-in sleeve template, and went about creating a collection of garments that were simultaneously a celebration of Walker's technique and a representation of the classic feminine styles I like best.

From a design perspective, creating pieces from the top down allowed for endless experimentation. I would simply drape incomplete garments over my dress form (or over myself), carefully consider what was working and what wasn't, and make changes accordingly. I felt encouraged to take chances but also to adhere closely to my own personal style. For me, that meant including a lot of dresses, which I wear more often than anything else. The first knitted dress I made was the Soho Smocked

Dress (page 29), which was inspired by the section in *Knitting from the Top* on adapting stitch patterns in the round. Top-down hats also proved to be a pure joy to knit and you'll find several versions here, such as the Pigeon Hat (page 61) and the Mulberry Hat (page 87). And then there were pieces born from sheer Walker-esque determination. The stitch pattern in the Seaport Skirt (page 65), for example, was inspired by my curiosity to see if I could mimic the effect of overlapping fish tails in a knitted form. I simply experimented with cables until I got it right. Of course, there were some quirky experiments, too, such as a pair of cotton underwear I created in order to better understand Walker's section on knitted pants. Although they deepened my understanding and appreciation of seamless construction (and were a riot to make), they did not make it into this collection.

While working my way through *Knitting from the Top* the first few times, I often found myself wishing that some of the trickier techniques were illustrated. For that reason, the first chapter of this book provides step-by-step photo tutorials of select techniques used in top-down construction, most of which are used in every garment presented here. The last chapter is dedicated to finishing. While top-down construction creates a smooth and polished end result as is, I like to spend a little extra time adding finishing touches, like sewing trim to hems and necklines, using elastic cord to add shaping, or crocheting decorative "seams" on the exterior of a dress. Implementing these extra steps to finish the pieces provides a sense of elegance and durability that helps to raise the garment to the next level, and the techniques required to do this are also explained in step-by-step photo tutorials.

All of the garments included in this book are written at set gauges and for predetermined sizes, but they can easily be adjusted to your liking simply by trying them on as you go and using common sense, and by following the customizing tips I've provided within the instructions. For those interested in taking a journey similar to the one that I took and learning more about designing their own garments, I heartily recommend the books listed on page 159. It is my greatest hope that some of the tips and techniques I have learned and incorporated into my patterns will spark individual creativity and exploration in others—much of what I've figured out is mercifully simple. And whether these techniques are brand new to you or something you've studied and enjoyed for a long time, I hope that I can impart even a small amount of the excitement and joy that went into creating the collection. As you explore your own knitting processes, I encourage you to remember these words that Walker shared with me: "Don't ever be afraid to experiment in knitting—trust yourself, you have nothing to lose."

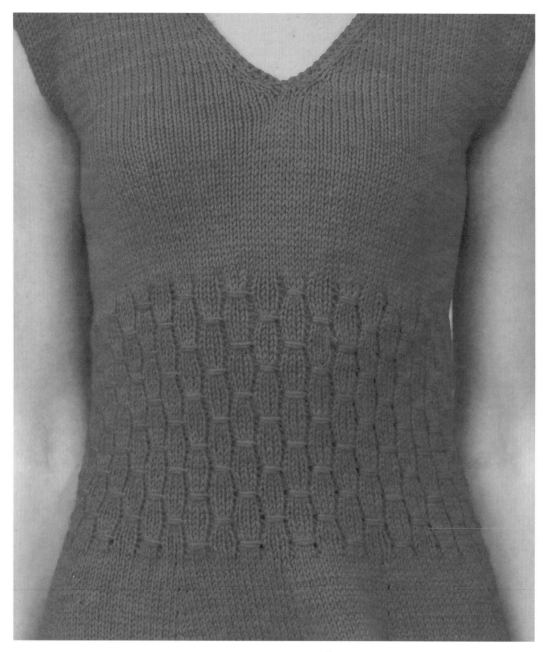

top-down tutorials

TOP-DOWN OVERVIEW

I created nearly every item in this book using knitting techniques that I learned from Barbara Walker's pioneering book, *Knitting from the Top*. And while Walker presents several different top-down styles (a classic raglan, a dropped-saddle shoulder, a kimono sleeve, and eleven types of pants—just to name a few!), the one I use for all of the sweaters and dresses in this collection (with the exception of the Blueberry Cardigan on page 111) is her seamless set-in sleeve design. This versatile, straightforward silhouette lends itself to countless incarnations and is quite simple to achieve. The garment is started at the shoulders using a provisional cast-on and the front and back are worked separately down to the bottom of the armholes. The front and back are then joined together on a circular needle, and the midriff and bottom are completed according to the pattern. If the item has sleeves, stitches are picked up around each armhole (again with a circular needle, or double-pointed needles) and are worked from the top down.

Working items from the top down in this way allows you a great deal of creative control over your work. You can easily adjust the length of your garment and its sleeves simply by knitting more or fewer rows, and you can place all of the stitches on a piece of waste yarn and slip the garment over your head at any stage of knitting to check the length and fit. This comes in handy for minor customizations, but can also help with bigger alterations, such as adding length to the bottom of a sweater to transform it into a dress and vice versa.

The top-down construction allows you to try on Jill's Dress (page 123) as you work so you can get the waist shaping and length just right.

In order to work the projects in this book from the top down, there are three key techniques you need to know—the provisional cast-on, short-row shoulder shaping, and setting in sleeves seamlessly. Following are step-by-step tutorials for each one.

PROVISIONAL CAST-ON

This technique allows you to cast on at the shoulders and work the back to the underarm, then go back to the cast-on row, pick up live stitches, and knit the front in the opposite direction. It creates no visible join or seam, and requires no sewing. Although there are several ways to work a provisional cast-on, the one I find easiest begins with a crocheted chain.

With a crochet hook and smooth waste yarn in a color that contrasts with your working yarn, chain the number of stitches needed for the cast-on, plus a few extra to keep the end from unraveling (**A**).

Flip the chain so its back side faces you (**B**). Insert the crochet hook through the back loops, and pull the working yarn through the loops and onto the hook (**C**). Once you have four or five stitches on your hook, slip them onto your needle (**D**). (Note that a knitting needle can be used instead of a crochet hook to work the first row of a provisional cast-on— you can experiment to see which technique works best for you.) Repeat until you have cast on as many stitches as you need.

With the working yarn, work as directed in the pattern, which, for the garment patterns in this book, always starts with the back. When you have finished the back section and are ready to work the front, carefully undo the first stitch of the crochet chain and pull the tail of the waste yarn (**E**). Load the live stitches onto your needle as they are released (**F**). You can now work in the opposite direction (the front of the garment) with the working yarn.

PROVISIONAL CAST-ON

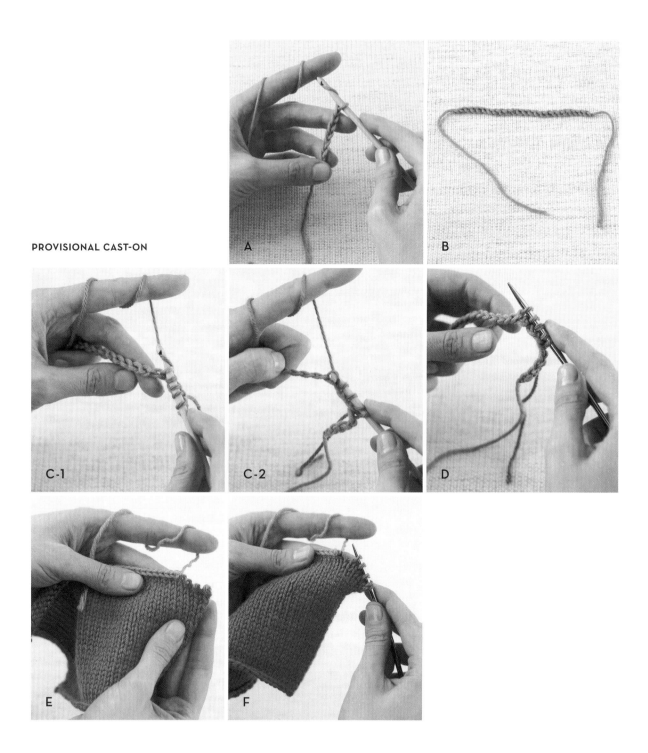

A

B

C-1

C-2

D

E

F

SHORT-ROW BASICS

When creating most of the garments in this book, there are two key places where you will need to work short rows: when you shape the shoulders (see page 21), and when you set in the sleeves (see page 22). Short rows are, essentially, rows that are worked back and forth between two set points to create extra height or a curve, allowing the fabric to fit the dimensions of the body gracefully. It's not imperative to work short rows (you can just knit straight through each section), but what you gain in fit makes the process worthwhile. The only time I don't bother with short rows is when the stitch pattern is too complicated and it becomes more trouble than it's worth. Following is the basic strategy for working short rows in Stockinette stitch.

Short rows in the Pavement Jacket (page 43) provide tailored curves at the shoulders and sleeve caps.

Working Short Rows on a Knit Row

1: Work the row for the specified number of stitches. In the example shown, I worked 4 stitches past the marker (**A**).

2: With the yarn in back, slip the next stitch as if to purl (**B**).

3: Bring the yarn to the front (**C**).

4: Slip the stitch from the right-hand needle back to the left-hand needle, and turn (wrp-t) (**D**). Work across the row as specified. Stitch will be wrapped (**E**).

**WORKING SHORT ROWS
ON A KNIT ROW**

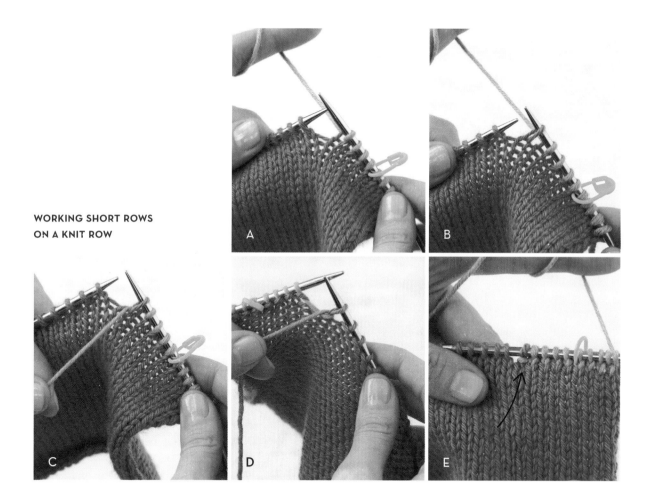

Working Short Rows on a Purl Row

1: Work the row for the specified number of stitches past the marker.

2: With the yarn in front, slip the next stitch as if to purl.

3: Bring the yarn to the back.

4: Slip the stitch from the right-hand needle back to the left-hand needle, and turn (wrp-t). Work across the row as specified. Stitch will be wrapped.

HIDING WRAPS

When working the row following a wrapped stitch, you must hide the wrap as you come to it. The method for doing this depends on whether you are purling or knitting a wrapped stitch.

Knitting a Wrapped Stitch: Insert the needle into the bottom of the wrap, from front to back (**F**), then knitwise into the stitch itself (**G**). Knit the wrap and the stitch together (**H**).

KNITTING A WRAPPED STITCH

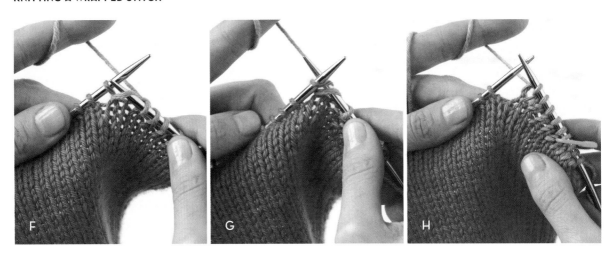

Purling a Wrapped Stitch: Insert the needle into the bottom of the wrap, from back to front (**I**), then purlwise into the stitch itself (**J**). Purl the wrap and the stitch together (**K**).

PURLING A WRAPPED STITCH

SHAPING SHOULDERS WITH SHORT ROWS

Working short rows at the shoulders helps to create a graceful curve and is done after working the provisional cast-on, starting with the back. Work a few rows and place two markers to indicate where your neck opening will be. Work short rows on either side of these markers at an interval specified in the pattern until you have reached the armhole edge. Continue working straight according to the pattern to just under the arm and put all of the back stitches on a piece of waste yarn.

To work the front, remove the provisional cast-on and load the live stitches onto your needle, placing the center neck stitches on waste yarn if instructed to do so. Work a row to bind off the center neck stitches if you have not placed them on waste yarn, then work short rows as you worked them for the back. (Remember that the two markers for the back indicated your neck opening and that for the front, these stitches are on a piece of waste yarn or bound off.) Work the stitches at intervals on either side of the neck opening with two separate balls of yarn, omitting the neck stitches. When the short rows are completed, work the front according to the pattern to just beneath the arm (to the same point as for the back) and connect the front and back onto one circular needle.

SET-IN, SEAMLESS, TOP-DOWN SLEEVES

Knitting sleeves from the top down creates a clean and fitted cap, allows you to adjust the finished length with ease, and best of all, requires no sewing. I used this type of construction for nearly all of the sleeves in this book.

Picking Up Stitches for the Sleeve

At any point after the front and back of the garment are connected and you've worked a few rows of the body, you can turn your attention to the sleeves. Join the yarn at the center of the underarm and pick up the required number of stitches evenly around the armhole. (Note: Barbara Walker instructs to calculate how many stitches are needed for the desired bicep circumference by multiplying that measurement by your gauge, rounding the number of stitches so they're divisible by two, and picking up this number of stitches evenly around the armhole. For the patterns presented here, these numbers have been provided.) Pick up stitches with a 16" circular needle (**A**). Place a marker at the beginning of the round (which is the bottom center of the armhole) and join.

**PICKING UP STITCHES
FOR THE SLEEVE**

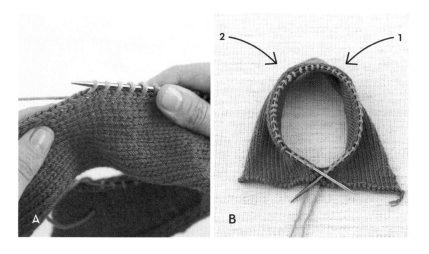

Creating Sleeve Cap with Short Rows

To shape the sleeve cap with short rows, starting clockwise, work the first right-side row for the number of stitches specified in the pattern (**B-1**) (this will always be approximately two-thirds of the way around the entire armhole), and, as described in the short-row section on page 19, wrap the next stitch and turn (wrp-t). Work the second row to the number of stitches specified in the pattern (**B-2**), wrap the next stitch and turn. Work back to the wrap from the previous row, hide the wrap, and then wrap and turn the next stitch. Continue back and forth in this manner, working short rows back and forth across the sleeve, taking one additional stitch from each side every time you make a turn. When all of the stitches (except those added at the underarm) have been worked, the cap is finished (**C**).

Work the final right-side row straight across the remaining underarm stitches (**D**). Hide the wrap that remains on the left side of the beginning-of-round marker as follows: Pick up the wrap with the right-hand needle from the bottom and knit it together with the stitch around which it was wrapped (**E**). Once this wrap is hidden, work the sleeve in the round as directed in the pattern, or as desired.

**CREATING SLEEVE CAP
WITH SHORT ROWS**

Tightening the Sleeve Pick-Up Round

Sometimes, when working set-in, seamless, top-down sleeves, the join where stitches are picked up and subsequently short-rowed can appear loose (**G**). If this happens, it is possible to tighten stitches around the edge of the sleeve by very carefully pulling on the pick-up tail (**H**), causing the sleeve and body to meet at a nice, more flush edge (**I**). Be careful not to tighten the pick-up tail too much or you may lose some elasticity in the picked-up edge.

PULL ON PICK-UP TAIL TO TIGHTEN JOIN

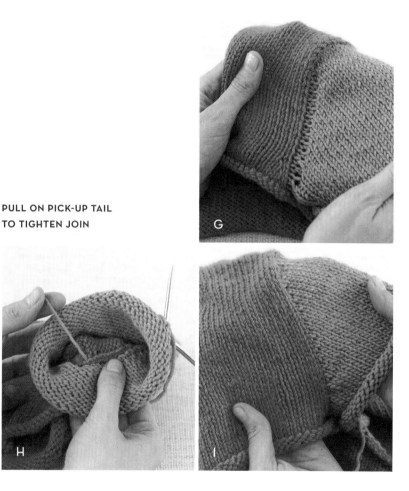

You can also use a crochet hook (or needle) to work out a loop that connects the two pieces at the pick-up round (**J**) and pull the loop to tighten (**K**). Make sure to hold on to the pick-up tail firmly when pulling the loop—if the pick-up tail is not secured, it is possible to pull it out and unravel the sleeve. When the join between sleeve and body is snug, cut the loop in half (**L**), tie the ends together on the wrong side, and weave them in to secure.

USE CROCHET HOOK TO TIGHTEN JOIN

the projects

soho smocked dress

Knitting is often full of surprises, and in this case, the surprise was discovering that I liked the wrong side of this dress (see page 33) as much as I liked the right side (see left). I'll leave it to you to choose which one you like best; then simply weave in the ends on the opposite side. The smocked stitch pattern I chose for the midriff hugs the body in an easy, flattering way, though the dress can easily be customized by substituting any stitch pattern worked in the round.

ABBREVIATION

Smock 5: Slip next 5 sts onto cn and hold in front of work; wrap yarn twice around sts on cn clockwise, then work the sts from cn as follows: p1, k3, p1.

STITCH PATTERN

Smocked Pattern
(multiple of 8 sts; 10-rnd repeat)

Note: The beginning of rnd stitch marker will be part of a group of sts to be smocked on Rnd 8; replace beginning of rnd marker after the first st once the group of 5 sts has been smocked.

RNDS 1 AND 2: *K3, p1; repeat from * around.

RND 3: *K3, smock 5; repeat from * around.

RNDS 4, 5, AND 6: Repeat Rnd 1.

RND 7: *K3, p1; repeat from * to last 4 sts, k3 (1 st remains before marker).

RND 8: Smock 5 (see Note), *k3, smock 5; repeat from * to last 4 sts, k3, p1.

RNDS 9 AND 10: Repeat Rnd 1.

Repeat Rnds 1–10 for Smocked Pattern.

sizes

X-Small (Small, Medium, Large, X-Large, 2X-Large)

finished measurements

31¼ (34½, 37½, 40¾, 44, 47¼)" bust

yarn

Shelridge Farm Soft Touch W4 (100% wool; 220 yards/100 grams): 8 (9, 10, 11, 12, 13) hanks Autumn Orange

needles

One 40" (100 cm) long circular (circ) needle size US 7 (4.5 mm)

One 24" (60 cm) long circular needle size US 7 (4.5 mm)

Change needle size if necessary to obtain correct gauge.

notions

Waste yarn; stitch markers; cable needle (cn); crochet hook size US G/6 (4 mm)

gauge

20 sts and 28 rows = 4" (10 cm) in Stockinette stitch (St st)

BACK

Using waste yarn, Provisional CO (see tutorial on page 16), and shorter circ needle, CO 76 (80, 84, 88, 92, 96) sts. Working in St st and beginning with a knit row, work 2 rows even.

NEXT ROW (RS): K19 (20, 21, 23, 24, 25), place marker (pm), k38 (40, 42, 42, 44, 46), pm, knit to end.

Shape Shoulders

ROWS 1 (WS) AND 2: Work to second marker, slip marker (sm), work 3 (3, 4, 4, 4, 5) sts, wrp-t (see tutorial on page 19).

ROWS 3–8: Work to wrapped st from row before previous row, hide wrap, work 3 (3, 3, 4, 4, 4) sts, wrp-t.

Work even in St st, hiding remaining wraps as you come to them, until armholes measure 7 ¼ (7, 7, 6 ¾, 6 ¼, 6 ¼)" from end of shoulder shaping, ending with a WS row.

Shape Armholes

INCREASE ROW (RS): Increase 1 st each side this row, then every other row 0 (2, 4, 6, 8, 10) times, as follows: K2, M1-R, knit to last 2 sts, M1, k2—78 (86, 94, 102, 110, 118) sts. Purl 1 WS row. Break yarn and set aside, leaving sts on needle.

FRONT

With RS facing, carefully unravel Provisional CO and place sts on longer circ needle for Front. Mark armhole edge for top of armhole.

NEXT ROW (RS): K19 (20, 21, 23, 24, 25); join a second ball of yarn, BO 38 (40, 42, 42, 44, 46) sts, knit to end.

Working BOTH SIDES AT THE SAME TIME using separate balls of yarn, shape shoulders as for Back, ending with a WS row. Work even in St st for 10 (10, 12, 14, 16, 16) rows, hiding remaining wraps as you come to them.

Shape Neck

Note: Neck and armhole shaping are worked at the same time; please read entire section through before beginning.

INCREASE ROW (RS): Increase 1 st each neck edge this row, then every other row 18 (19, 20, 18, 19, 20) times, as follows: On right neck edge, knit to last 2 sts, M1-R, k2; on left neck edge, k2, M1, knit to end. Purl 1 WS row.

AT THE SAME TIME, when Front measures same as for Back from marker to beginning of armhole shaping, shape armholes as for Back, ending with a WS row. Break yarn for right Front.

BODY

Join Back to Fronts

With RS facing, transfer Back sts to right-hand end of circ needle. Your sts should now be in the following order, from right to left, with RS facing: Back, right Front, left Front. Using yarn attached to left Front, pm for left side seam, work across Back sts, pm for right side seam, then work across

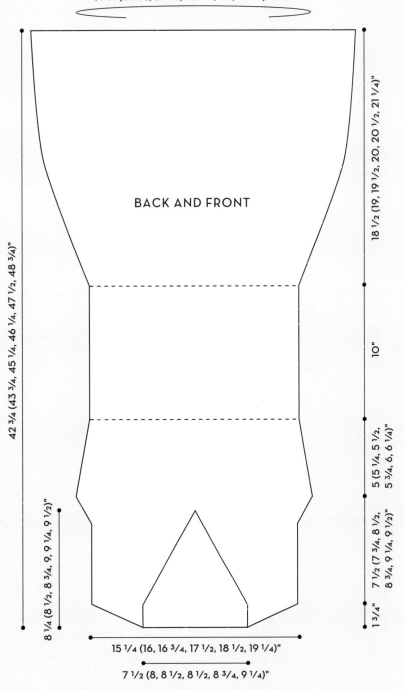

46 ¾ (50, 52 ¾, 57 ½, 59 ¾, 64 ½)" hips

28 ¾ (32, 35 ¼, 38 ½, 41 ½, 44 ¾)" waist

31 ¼ (34 ½, 37 ½, 40 ¾, 44, 47 ¼)" bust

BACK AND FRONT

18 ½ (19, 19 ½, 20, 20 ½, 21 ¼)"

10"

5 (5 ¼, 5 ½, 5 ¾, 6, 6 ¼)"

7 ½ (7 ¾, 8 ½, 8 ¾, 9 ¼, 9 ½)"

1 ¾"

42 ¾ (43 ¾, 45 ¼, 46 ¼, 47 ½, 48 ¾)"

8 ¼ (8 ½, 8 ¾, 9, 9 ¼, 9 ½)"

15 ¼ (16, 16 ¾, 17 ½, 18 ½, 19 ¼)"

7 ½ (8, 8 ½, 8 ½, 8 ¾, 9 ¼)"

right Front sts. Do not join. Purl 1 WS row. Continue working increases at neck edges if necessary, until you have a total of 156 (172, 188, 204, 220, 236) sts, ending with a WS row.

Join Fronts

NEXT ROW (RS): Work to end. Join for working in the rnd; work to second marker (this will now be beginning of rnd marker). Work even until piece measures 2 (2 ¼, 2 ½, 2 ¾, 3, 3 ¼)" from armholes.

Shape Waist

DECREASE RND 1: *K37 (41, 45, 49, 53, 57), k2tog; repeat from * to end—152 (168, 184, 200, 216, 232) sts remain. Work 9 rnds even.

DECREASE RND 2: *K36 (40, 44, 48, 52, 56), k2tog; repeat from * to end—148 (164, 180, 196, 212, 228) sts remain. Work 9 rnds even.

DECREASE RND 3: *K35 (39, 43, 47, 51, 55), k2tog; repeat from * to end—144 (160, 176, 192, 208, 224) sts remain.

✳ *Customizing Tip:* You may wish to transfer your stitches to waste yarn and try the piece on at this point, before beginning the Smocked Pattern. The piece should sit comfortably below your bustline. Work additional rounds if necessary to ensure proper fit. If you find that it is longer than you would like, consider reworking the preceding Decrease Rounds, working fewer rounds between each decrease. ✳

NEXT RND: Work Rnds 1-10 of Smocked Pattern 5 times, then Rnds 1-5 once.

Shape Hip

NEXT RND: *K16, pm; repeat from * around. Total of 9 (10, 11, 12, 13, 14) markers placed.

INCREASE RND: Increase 9 (10, 11, 12, 13, 14) sts this rnd, then every 5 (6, 7, 7, 8, 8) rnds 9 (8, 7, 7, 6, 6) times, as follows: *Knit to 1 st before marker, k1-f/b; repeat from * to end—234 (250, 264, 288, 299, 322) sts. Work even until piece measures 18 ½ (19, 19 ½, 20, 20 ½, 21 ¼) from bodice. BO all sts.

FINISHING

✳ *Customizing Tip:* If you wish to add sleeves to the dress (¾-length sleeves would look especially nice), use a 16" circular needle in the same size you used to work the piece, and following the tutorial on page 22, pick up and knit stitches around the armhole edge and work down, shaping the sleeve to the desired length and width. If you want to work a few rounds of the Smocked Pattern for the cuff, just make sure you have a multiple of 8 stitches before you begin the pattern. Then finish off the cuff with 1 rnd sc (see tutorial on page 150). ✳

Using crochet hook, work 1 rnd sc (see tutorial on page 150) around armholes and neckline, working 1 sc in every other row at neck edges and around armholes. Work 2 rnds sc along bottom edge. Weave in all ends. Block as desired.

pleated
arm warmers

My grandmother gave me a pair of elbow-length navy blue silk gloves when I was in high school. Though I found few occasions to wear them, putting them on always made me feel rather elegant—a feeling I have tried to capture here in this knitted version. I used a silky-smooth bamboo yarn and a pleated pattern that feels nice around the hands and layers perfectly under any coat.

ABBREVIATION

Tuck: Insert tip of right-hand needle in next st knitwise, pick up corresponding st 7 rows below, and knit the 2 sts together.

STITCH PATTERN

Tuck Pattern

(multiple of 8 sts; 16-rnd repeat)

RND 1: K4, *tuck 4, k4; repeat from * to last 4 sts, tuck 4.

RNDS 2-7: Knit.

RND 8: *Tuck 4, k4; repeat from * around.

RNDS 9-16: Knit.

Repeat Rnds 1-16 for Tuck Pattern.

sizes
Small (Large)

finished measurements
5 ¾ (6 ¾)" palm circumference
24" long

yarn
Be Sweet Bamboo (100% bamboo; 115 yards/50 grams): 4 (5) balls #661 Midnight

needles
One set of four double-pointed needles (dpn) size US 4 (3.5 mm)
Change needle size if necessary to obtain correct gauge.

notions
Stitch marker; crochet hook size US E/4 (3.5 mm)

gauge
14 sts and 19 rnds = 2" (5 cm) in Stockinette stitch (St st)

HAND

CO 40 (48) sts. Distribute among 3 dpns as follows: 12-12-16 (16-16-16). Place marker (pm) for beginning of rnd and join, being careful not to twist sts. Knit 9 rnds.

Begin Pattern

Work Rnds 1-16 of Tuck Pattern 3 times (piece should measure approximately 2").

Thumb Opening

RND 1: BO 8 (10) sts, knit to end.

RND 2: CO 8 (10) sts, knit to end.

Work Rnds 1-16 of Tuck Pattern 3 more times (piece should measure approximately 5½"). ✳ *Customizing Tip:* If you prefer to make the Arm Warmers shorter, simply BO at this point and proceed to Finishing. ✳ Work even in St st for 5¼ (6)" from end of Tuck Pattern.

ARM

INCREASE RND 1: K10 (8), M1, *k6 (8), M1; repeat from * 4 times—46 (54) sts. Work even for 6" from Increase Rnd 1.

INCREASE RND 2: K6 (9), M1, *k8 (9), M1; repeat from * 4 times—52 (60) sts.

Work even for 7", or to desired length from Increase Rnd 2. BO all sts.

FINISHING

Using crochet hook, work 1 rnd sc (see tutorial on page 150) around CO edge and thumb opening. Weave in all ends. Block as desired.

subway hat

One freezing afternoon in New York City, I struck up a conversation with a woman on the subway who was wearing an old wool ski hat that she had cut up the back so that it framed her head like a bonnet. She told me that she had simply wanted the hat out of her eyes and to fall more comfortably around her ears. Inspired by the fit she achieved, I came up with this top-down knitted version in a cheery pumpkin color. I then lined the inside with fleece—a simple step that adds warmth and structure.

NOTE

✳ When starting the Hat, you may find it easier to work on 3 double-pointed needles (dpns) than on 4. Adjust stitch positions accordingly and change to 4 dpns when there are enough stitches to fit comfortably. Change to circular needle when there are enough stitches to fit on the needle.

CROWN

CO 8 sts. Distribute evenly among 4 dpns; place marker (pm) for beginning of rnd and join, being careful not to twist sts.

Shape Crown

RND 1: *K1-f/b; repeat from * to end—16 sts.

RND 2: *K2, pm; repeat from * to last 2 sts, k2—7 markers placed in addition to beginning of rnd marker.

INCREASE RND: Increase 8 sts this rnd, every other rnd 3 (4, 5) times, then every 5 rnds twice, as follows: *K1-f/b, knit to marker, slip marker (sm); repeat from * to end—64 (72, 80) sts.

Work even in St st until piece measures 1" from last increase, removing all 7 shaping markers on first rnd.

size
Small (Medium, Large)

finished measurements
18 ¼ (20 ½, 22 ¾)" head circumference

yarn
Blue Sky Alpacas Worsted Hand Dyes (50% alpaca/50% merino wool; 100 yards/100 grams): 1 (2, 2) hanks #2010 Rusty Orange

needles
One set of five double-pointed needles (dpn) size US 10 ½ (6.5 mm)

One 16" (40 cm) long circular (circ) needle size US 10 ½ (6.5 mm)

Change needle size if necessary to obtain correct gauge.

notions
Stitch marker; crochet hook size US K/10 ½ (6.5 mm); tapestry needle; 20" square fleece, for lining; sewing needle and matching thread

gauge
14 sts and 22 rnds = 4" (10 cm) in Stockinette stitch (St st)

Fleece lining is sewn to the inside of this hat, adding warmth and providing structure to the finished piece.

Work Back Opening

NEXT ROW: Knit to marker, turn. Continue working back and forth in St st for 6 (6 ¼, 6 ½)". BO all sts.

FINISHING

Thread CO tail onto tapestry needle and pull through 8 CO sts. Pull tightly and secure. Using crochet hook, work 2 rows sc (see tutorial on page 150) in every other row along back opening. Work 2 rows sc along front edge.

Weave in all ends. Block as desired.

Cut 2 pieces of fleece to match the right and left inside portions of the hat and sew the edges of the fleece neatly along the bottom inside edges of the hat using the last round of sc as a guide. Sew down the top middle edges on each side of the fleece to attach them to the hat and to each other.

pavement jacket

For the body of this tailored jacket, I chose a simple stitch pattern with a rough, pavement-like texture, which is accentuated by simple Garter stitch sleeves. The top-down technique is especially useful for customizing sleeve length, which in this case I kept on the long side. Heavy-duty sew-on snaps finish the look, enhancing the functionality of this cold-weather staple.

STITCH PATTERNS

Shadow 2x1 Rib
(multiple of 3 sts + 2; 2-row repeat)
ROW 1 (WS): Knit.
ROW 2: P2, *k1-tbl, p2; repeat from * to end.
Repeat Rows 1 and 2 for Shadow 2x1 Rib.

Shadow 3x1 Rib
(multiple of 4 sts + 3; 2-row repeat)
ROW 1 (WS): Knit.
ROW 2: P3, *k1-tbl, p3; repeat from * to end.
Repeat Rows 1 and 2 for Shadow 3x1 Rib.

Twisted Garter Stitch
(any number of sts; 1-row repeat)
ALL ROWS: *K1-tbl; repeat from * to end.

NOTE
✳ After the initial Provisional CO, use Backward Loop CO for any other COs in this pattern (see Special Techniques, page 157).

sizes
X-Small (Small, Medium, Large, X-Large, 2X-Large)

finished measurements
34 (37 3/4, 40 3/4, 44 1/2, 49, 52 3/4)" bust, buttoned

yarn
Botto Paola New Relax (100% merino wool; 546 yards/1 pound): 1805 (2085, 2380, 2660, 2960, 3295) yards #701 Grigio

needles
One 16" (40 cm) long circular (circ) needle size US 7 (4.5 mm)

One 32" (80 cm) long circular needle size US 7 (4.5 mm)

One set of five double-pointed needles (dpn) size US 7 (4.5 mm)

Change needle size if necessary to obtain correct gauge.

notions
Waste yarn; stitch markers; stitch holders; 11 size-10 sew-on snaps; 11 size-24 capped prong ring snaps to match; snap-affixing hardware; crochet hook size US G/6 (4 mm)

gauge
19 sts and 25 rows = 4" (10 cm) in Shadow 2x1 Rib

18 sts and 30 rows = 4" (10 cm) in Garter st (knit every row)

BACK

Using waste yarn, Provisional CO (see tutorial on page 16) and shorter circ needle, CO 71 (77, 80, 86, 89, 95) sts. Work Row 1 of Shadow 2x1 Rib.

NEXT ROW (RS): Working in pattern, work 20 (23, 23, 26, 26, 29) sts, place marker (pm), work 31 (31, 34, 34, 37, 37) sts, pm, work to end.

Shape Shoulders

ROWS 1 (WS) AND 2: Work to second marker, slip marker (sm), work 4 (3, 3, 5, 5, 5) sts, wrp-t (see tutorial on page 19).

ROWS 3–8: Work to wrapped st from row before previous row, hide wrap, work 3 (4, 4, 4, 4, 5) sts, wrp-t.

Work even, hiding remaining wraps as you come to them, until armholes measure 7 (7¼, 7¼, 8, 8, 8¼)" from end of shoulder shaping, ending with RS row.

Shape Armholes

INCREASE ROW (WS): Increase 1 st each edge this row, then every other row 2 (2, 4, 5, 7, 8) times, as follows, working new sts into pattern: K2, M1, knit to last 2 sts, M1, k2—77 (83, 90, 98, 105, 113) sts. Break yarn and set aside, leaving sts on needle for Body.

FRONT

With RS facing, carefully unravel Provisional CO and place first and last 20 (23, 23, 26, 26, 29) sts on longer circ needle for Front. Leave center 31 (31, 34, 34, 37, 37) sts on waste yarn for Back neck. Mark armhole edge for top of armhole. Working BOTH SIDES AT THE SAME TIME using separate balls of yarn, work Row 2 of Shadow 2x1 Rib. Shape shoulders as for Back.

Work even, hiding remaining wraps as you come to them, until neck edge measures 4 (4¼, 4½, 5, 5¼, 5½)", ending with a WS row.

Shape Neck

ROW 1 (RS): On Right Front, work to end, CO 15 (15, 15, 15, 18, 18) sts; on Left Front, work to end.

ROW 2: On Left Front, work to end, CO 15 (15, 15, 15, 18, 18) sts; on Right Front, work to end—35 (38, 38, 41, 44, 47) sts each Front.

Work even until piece measures same as for Back from marker to beginning of armhole shaping. Shape armholes as for Back, ending with a RS row for Left Front and a WS row for Right Front—38 (41, 43, 47, 52, 56) sts each Front. Break yarn for Right Front. Do not turn Left Front.

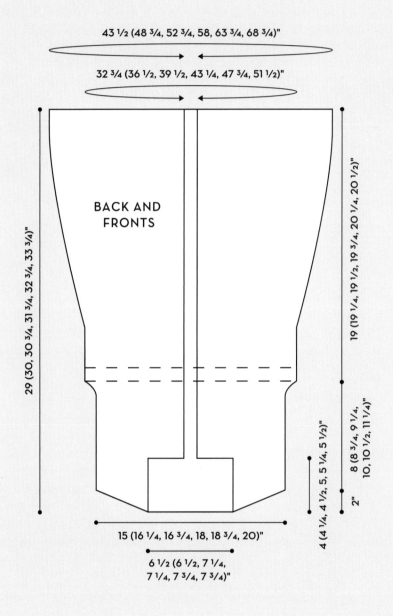

43 1/2 (48 3/4, 52 3/4, 58, 63 3/4, 68 3/4)"

32 3/4 (36 1/2, 39 1/2, 43 1/4, 47 3/4, 51 1/2)"

BACK AND FRONTS

29 (30, 30 3/4, 31 3/4, 32 3/4, 33 3/4)"

19 (19 1/4, 19 1/2, 19 3/4, 20 1/4, 20 1/2)"

8 (8 3/4, 9 1/4, 10, 10 1/2, 11 1/4)"

4 (4 1/4, 4 1/2, 5, 5 1/4, 5 1/2)"

2"

15 (16 1/4, 16 3/4, 18, 18 3/4, 20)"

6 1/2 (6 1/2, 7 1/4, 7 1/4, 7 3/4, 7 3/4)"

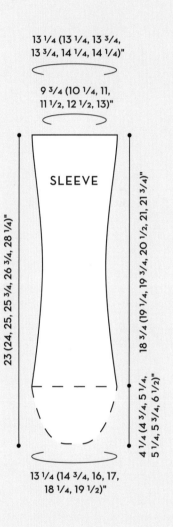

13 1/4 (13 1/4, 13 3/4, 13 3/4, 14 1/4, 14 1/4)"

9 3/4 (10 1/4, 11, 11 1/2, 12 1/2, 13)"

SLEEVE

23 (24, 25, 25 3/4, 26 3/4, 28 1/4)"

18 3/4 (19 1/4, 19 3/4, 20 1/2, 21, 21 3/4)"

4 1/4 (4 3/4, 5 1/4, 5 1/4, 5 3/4, 6 1/2)"

13 1/4 (14 3/4, 16, 17, 18 1/4, 19 1/2)"

BODY

Join Back to Fronts

With RS facing, transfer Right Front sts (turned so that RS is facing) then Back sts to right-hand end of circ needle. Your sts should now be in the following order, from right to left, with RS facing: Back, Right Front, Left Front. Using yarn attached to Left Front, CO 0 (2, 3, 3, 4, 5) sts for underarm, pm for left side, CO 1 (2, 3, 4, 5, 5) st(s), work across Back sts, CO 1 (2, 3, 4, 5, 5) st(s) for underarm, pm for right side, CO 0 (2, 3, 3, 4, 5) sts, work across Right Front sts—155 (173, 188, 206, 227, 245) sts. ✳ *Customizing Tip:* You may wish to transfer your stitches to waste yarn and try the piece on at this point, before beginning the Twisted Garter stitch band. The piece should sit comfortably below your bustline. Work additional rows if necessary to ensure proper fit. ✳ Work 12 rows in Twisted Garter stitch. Change back to Shadow 2x1 Rib and work even until piece measures 3" from underarm, ending with a RS row.

Shape Hip

INCREASE ROW (WS): *K1, M1-R, k2; repeat from * to last 2 sts, k1, M1, k1—207 (231, 251, 275, 303, 327) sts. Change to Shadow 3x1 Rib and work even until piece measures 19 (19 1/4, 19 1/2, 19 3/4, 20 1/4, 20 1/2)" from underarm, ending with a WS row. BO all sts.

SLEEVES

With RS facing, using shorter circ needle, and beginning at center of underarm, pick up and knit 60 (66, 72, 76, 82, 88) sts evenly around armhole (see tutorial on page 22). Pm for beginning of rnd and join.

Shape Cap

ROW 1 (RS): K38 (42, 46, 48, 52, 56), wrp-t.

ROW 2: K16 (18, 20, 20, 22, 24), wrp-t.

ROWS 3 AND 4: Work to wrapped st from row before previous row, hide wrap, wrp-t.

Repeat Rows 3 and 4 fourteen (16, 18, 18, 20, 22) times. Change to Garter st in-the-rnd (knit 1 rnd, purl 1 rnd) and work even for 1".

Shape Upper Sleeve

Note: Change to dpns when necessary for number of sts on needle.

DECREASE RND: Decrease 2 sts this rnd, every 8 (6, 6, 6, 6, 4) rnds 5 (4, 7, 10, 12, 4) times, then every 10 (8, 8, 8, 8, 6) rnds 2 (5, 3, 1, 0, 10) time(s), as follows: K2tog, knit to last 2 sts, ssk—44 (46, 50, 52, 56, 58) sts remain. Work even until piece measures 9 (9 1/4, 9 1/2, 9 3/4, 10 1/4, 10 1/2)" from underarm.

Shape Lower Sleeve

INCREASE RND: Increase 2 sts this rnd, every 8 (10, 12, 16, 20, 28) rnds 3 (4, 3, 4, 3, 2) times, then every 10 (12, 14, 0, 0, 0) rnds 4 (2, 2, 0, 0, 0) times, as follows, working new sts into pattern: Work 1, M1, work to last st, M1, work 1—60 (60, 62, 62, 64, 64) sts. Work even until sleeve measures 18 3/4 (19 1/4, 19 3/4, 20 1/2, 21, 21 3/4)" from underarm. BO all sts.

FINISHING

Collar

With RS facing, using longer circ needle, pick up and knit 35 (36, 38, 39, 44, 46) sts along Right Front neck, 31 (31, 34, 34, 37, 37) sts along Back neck, and 35 (36, 38, 39, 44, 46) sts along Left Front neck—101 (103, 110, 112, 125, 129) sts. Work even in Garter st until collar measures 4", or to desired length. BO all sts. Using crochet hook, work 1 row sc (see tutorial on page 150) along BO edge.

Bands

With RS facing, using longer circ needle, pick up and knit 113 (115, 118, 120, 122, 125) sts along Right Front edge. Work even in Garter st for 8 rows. BO all sts. Repeat along Left Front edge.

Hem Edging

Using crochet hook, work 2 rows sc along bottom edge. Attach capped prong rings and matching sockets to Right Front, the first and last snaps ¾" from top and bottom edges, and the remaining 9 evenly spaced between. Do not attach the studs to the Left Front; they will not be used. Sew half of each sew-on snap to the back of each capped prong ring socket, and the opposite half of each snap to the RS of the Left Front.

Weave in all ends. Block as desired.

layered ruffle sweater

The ruffles on this sweater are easy to make and highlight a flattering, low neckline. Worked as separate panels with elastic cord crocheted into the top edges, they are sewn onto the body of the garment in layers. To turn the sweater into a dress, simply add length at the bottom and finish with several rows of single crochet at the hem.

NOTE

✳ After the initial Provisional CO, use Backward Loop CO for any other COs in this pattern (see Special Techniques, page 157).

BACK

Using waste yarn and Provisional CO (see tutorial on page 16), CO 82 (90, 94, 96, 98, 100, 102) sts. Working in St st and beginning with a knit row, work 1 row even.

NEXT ROW (WS): P15 (18, 20, 20, 21, 21, 22), place marker (pm), p52 (54, 54, 56, 56, 58, 58), pm, purl to end.

Shape Shoulders

ROWS 1 (RS) AND 2: Work to second marker, slip marker (sm), work 5 (6, 6, 6, 7, 7, 8) sts, wrp-t (see tutorial on page 19).

ROWS 3 AND 4: Work to wrapped st from row before previous row, hide wrap, work 4 (5, 6, 6, 6, 6, 6) sts, wrp-t.

Work even in St st, hiding remaining wraps as you come to them, until piece measures 6¼ (7¼, 7¼, 7¼, 7½, 7½, 7½)" from end of shoulder shaping, ending with a WS row.

sizes

X-Small (Small, Medium, Large, X-Large, 2X-Large, 3X-Large)

finished measurements

32 (35, 37 ¾, 40 ¾, 43 ¾, 46 ½, 49 ½)" bust

yarn

Filatura di Crosa Zara (100% merino wool; 137 yards/50 grams): 7 (8, 9, 9, 10, 11, 12) balls #431 True Green

needles

One 24" (60 cm) long circular (circ) needle size US 4 (3.5 mm)

Change needle size if necessary to obtain correct gauge.

notions

Waste yarn; stitch markers; crochet hook size US E/4 (3.5 mm); 2 yards thin, round elastic cord

gauge

22 sts and 31 rows = 4" (10 cm) in Stockinette stitch (St st)

Shape Armholes

INCREASE ROW (RS): Increase 1 st each side this row, then every other row 2 (2, 2, 4, 5, 7, 8) times, as follows: K2, M1-R, knit to last 2 sts, M1, k2—88 (96, 100, 106, 110, 116, 120) sts. Purl 1 WS row. Break yarn and transfer sts to waste yarn for Body.

FRONT

With RS facing, carefully unravel Provisional CO and place sts on circ needle for Front. Mark armhole edge for top of armhole.

NEXT ROW (RS): K15 (18, 20, 20, 21, 21, 22) sts; join a second ball of yarn, BO 52 (54, 54, 56, 56, 58, 58) sts, knit to end. Working BOTH SIDES AT THE SAME TIME using separate balls of yarn, purl 1 row. Shape shoulders as for Back. Work even, hiding remaining wraps as you come to them, until neck edge measures 2½ (2¾, 2½, 2¾, 2¾, 2¾, 2¼)", ending with a WS row.

Shape Neck

Note: Neck and armhole shaping are worked at the same time; please read entire section through before beginning.

INCREASE ROW (RS): Increase 1 st each neck edge this row, then every other row 22 (23, 25, 26, 28, 30, 32) times, as follows: On right Front, knit to last 2 sts, M1-R, k2; on left Front, k2, M1, knit to end. AT THE SAME TIME, when armholes measure same as for Back from marker to beginning of armhole shaping, shape armholes as for Back, ending with a WS row—41 (45, 49, 52, 56, 60, 64) sts each side when neck and armhole shaping are complete. Break yarn for right Front.

BODY

Join Back and Fronts

With RS facing, transfer Back sts, then right Front sts to left-hand end of circ needle. Your sts should now be in the following order, from right to left, with RS facing: left Front, Back, right Front. Using yarn attached to left Front, knit across left Front sts, CO 0 (0, 1, 1, 2, 3, 4) st(s) for underarm, pm for left side and beginning of rnd, CO 0 (0, 1, 2, 3, 3, 4) st(s), knit across Back sts, CO 0 (0, 1, 1, 2, 3, 4) st(s) for underarm, pm for right side, CO 0 (0, 1, 2, 3, 3, 4) st(s), knit across right Front sts, CO 6 (6, 6, 8, 8, 8, 8) sts for center Front, knit to beginning of rnd—176 (192, 208, 224, 240, 256, 272) sts. Work even in St st until piece measures 2" from underarm.

Shape Bust

DECREASE RND: Decrease 4 sts this rnd, then every other rnd twice, as follows: [Ssk, work to 2 sts before marker, k2tog, slip marker (sm)] twice—164 (180, 196, 212, 228, 244, 260) sts remain. Work even until piece measures 12¾" from underarm. ✳ *Customizing Tip:* The hip shaping takes approximately 4¼" to complete, followed by 2" with no shaping. You may wish to transfer your stitches to waste yarn and try the piece on well before the point at which you are to begin the hip shaping. Determine how much longer you want the finished piece to be, and begin the hip shaping 6¼" from that length. ✳

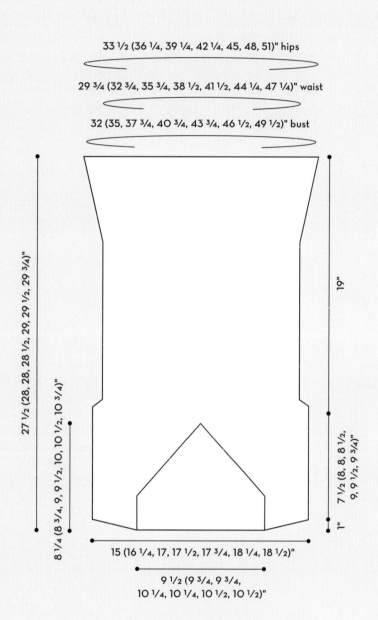

33 ½ (36 ¼, 39 ¼, 42 ¼, 45, 48, 51)" hips

29 ¾ (32 ¾, 35 ¾, 38 ½, 41 ½, 44 ¼, 47 ¼)" waist

32 (35, 37 ¾, 40 ¾, 43 ¾, 46 ½, 49 ½)" bust

27 ½ (28, 28, 28 ½, 29, 29 ½, 29 ¾)"

8 ¼ (8 ¾, 9, 9 ½, 10, 10 ½, 10 ¾)"

19"

7 ½ (8, 8, 8 ½, 9, 9 ½, 9 ¾)"

1"

15 (16 ¼, 17, 17 ½, 17 ¾, 18 ¼, 18 ½)"

9 ½ (9 ¾, 9 ¾, 10 ¼, 10 ¼, 10 ½, 10 ½)"

Note: Dotted lines represent placement of Ruffles.

Shape Hip

INCREASE RND: Increase 4 sts this rnd, then every 8 rnds 4 times, as follows: [K1-f/b, knit to 1 st before marker, k1-f/b, sm] twice—184 (200, 216, 232, 248, 264, 280) sts. Work even until piece measures 19" from underarm. BO all sts.

FINISHING

Wide Ruffle

CO 98 (110, 116, 130, 142, 154, 160) sts. Work back and forth in St st until piece measures 2¾". BO all sts. Using crochet hook, work 1 row sc (see tutorial on page 150) along 3 sides of piece, working 1 sc into each st on CO edge, and 1 sc into approximately 3 out of every 4 rows on side edges, leaving BO edge free.

Medium Ruffle

CO 72 (78, 84, 90, 96, 102, 108) sts. Complete as for Wide Ruffle.

Narrow Ruffle

CO 42 (46, 50, 54, 58, 62, 66) sts. Complete as for Wide Ruffle.

Block pieces.

Gather Ruffle

With RS facing, using crochet hook and holding elastic cord parallel to BO edge, work 1 row sc around BO edge and cord, working cord into sc (see tutorial on page 155). Gently pull ends of elastic to create ruffle, cinching the Wide and Medium Ruffles to approximately half their original width, and the Narrow Ruffle to approximately two-thirds its original width. Tie ends of elastic to sides to secure, and weave in ends. Center Wide Ruffle along neckline (with gathered edge along neck edge) so that the sides end approximately 4" below shoulders; sew in place. Center Medium Ruffle parallel to neck edge, placed approximately ¾" below Wide Ruffle; sew in place. Center Narrow Ruffle parallel to neck edge, placed approximately 2" below Medium Ruffle; sew in place. Work 1 rnd sc around neckline, armholes, and bottom edge, working 1 sc into each CO or BO st, and 1 sc into approximately 3 out of every 4 rows along vertical edges. Weave in all ends.

suspension dress

The stitch pattern in the bodice of this dress reminds me of the cables in suspension bridges, especially when worked in a silvery-gray yarn. Initially, I designed the dress to be strapless and sewed an elastic band to the upper inside edge of the bodice to secure the fit. I found the look charming, though doubts about the practicality of a knitted strapless dress ultimately led me to attach the top band, shown here. I finished the top and bottom inside edges with a beautiful light-gray lace trim (see page 59).

STITCH PATTERN

Slip Stitch Pattern
(multiple of 3 sts; 2-rnd repeat)
RND 1: *P1, slip 2 wyif; repeat from * to end.
RND 2: Knit.
Repeat Rnds 1 and 2 for Slip Stitch Pattern.

NOTE

✳ For best fit, select a size 6-8" smaller than actual bust measurement.

BODICE

With 2 strands of yarn held together, CO 87 (99, 111, 120, 132, 144) sts. Place marker (pm) for beginning of rnd and join, being careful not to twist sts. Work in Slip Stitch Pattern until piece measures approximately 10¼ (10¾, 11, 11¼, 11½, 12)" from the beginning, ending with Rnd 2 of Slip Stitch Pattern, increase 1 (0, 0, 1, 0, 0) or decrease 0 (0, 1, 0, 0, 1) st(s) on last rnd—88 (99, 110, 121, 132, 143) sts.
NEXT RND: *K8 (9, 10, 11, 12, 13), pm; repeat from * to end.

sizes

X-Small (Small, Medium, Large, X-Large, 2X-Large)

finished measurements

26 (29½, 33, 35½, 39, 42½)" bust

yarn

Filatura di Crosa Zara (100% merino wool; 137 yards/50 grams): 14 (15, 17, 19, 21, 23) balls #1494 Light Gray

needles

One 24" (60 cm) long circular (circ) needle size US 10½ (6.5 mm)

One 40" (100 cm) long circular needle size US 10½ (6.5 mm)

Change needle size if necessary to obtain correct gauge.

notions

Stitch markers; crochet hook size US K/10½ (6.5 mm); tapestry needle; 3 yards 1"-wide lace or trim; sewing needle and matching thread

gauge

13½ sts and 33 rnds = 4" (10 cm) in Slip Stitch Pattern

13 sts and 20 rnds = 4" (10 cm) in Stockinette stitch (St st) with 2 strands of yarn held together

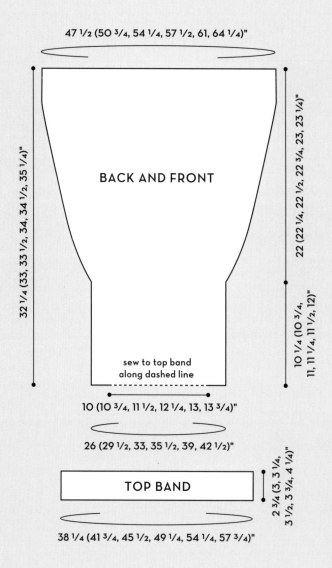

47 1/2 (50 3/4, 54 1/4, 57 1/2, 61, 64 1/4)"

BACK AND FRONT

32 1/4 (33, 33 1/2, 34, 34 1/2, 35 1/4)"

22 (22 1/4, 22 1/2, 22 3/4, 23, 23 1/4)"

10 1/4 (10 3/4, 11, 11 1/4, 11 1/2, 12)"

sew to top band
along dashed line

10 (10 3/4, 11 1/2, 12 1/4, 13, 13 3/4)"

26 (29 1/2, 33, 35 1/2, 39, 42 1/2)"

TOP BAND

2 3/4 (3, 3 1/4,
3 1/2, 3 3/4, 4 1/4)"

38 1/4 (41 3/4, 45 1/2, 49 1/4, 54 1/4, 57 3/4)"

SKIRT

Note: Change to longer circ needle when necessary for number of sts on needle.

Shape Skirt

INCREASE RND: Increase 11 sts this rnd, then every 5 (5, 6, 6, 7, 8) rnds 5 times, as follows: *Knit to 1 st before marker, k1-f/b; repeat from * to end —154 (165, 176, 187, 198, 209) sts. Work even in St st until piece measures 22 (22 ¼, 22 ½, 22 ¾, 23, 23 ¼)" from beginning of Skirt. BO all sts.

TOP BAND

With 2 strands of yarn held together, using long circ needle, CO 124 (136, 148, 160, 176, 188) sts. Pm for beginning of rnd and join, being careful not to twist sts. Work in St st for 2 ¾ (3, 3 ¼, 3 ½, 3 ¾, 4 ¼)". BO all sts. Using crochet hook and 2 strands of yarn held together, work 1 rnd sc (see tutorial on page 150) along CO and BO edges of Band.

FINISHING

With RS facing, center Top Band along top of Dress and, using single strand of yarn threaded on tapestry needle, sew Band to front and back for 10 (10 ¼, 11 ½, 12 ¼, 13, 13 ¾)", leaving 3 (4, 5, 5 ½, 6 ½, 7 ½)" of Bodice open on either side for arms. Using needle and thread, sew trim to top edge of Band on WS (see tutorial on page 149). Using crochet hook and 2 strands of yarn held together, work 2 rnds sc along bottom edge of Dress. Sew lace or trim to WS of hem. Weave in all ends. Block as desired.

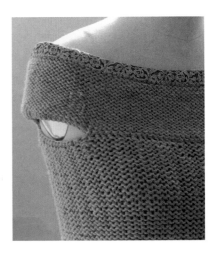

Lace trim sewn to the inside neck edge and hem adds an heirloom quality to the dress.

pigeon hat

I dyed the yarn for this hat to mimic the coloring of pigeons, which I see every day in Brooklyn. I worked the hat from the top down using a fine gauge alpaca yarn in cream, and then painted it with Jacquard acid dye in silver gray, gun metal, and jet black. The result is a sleek and sophisticated piece that is easy to personalize and make your own. Just as no two pigeons are exactly alike, no two versions of this hat will be either.

NOTE

⁑ When starting the Hat, you may find it easier to work on 3 double-pointed needles (dpns) than on 4. Adjust stitch positions accordingly and change to 4 dpns when there are enough stitches to fit comfortably. Change to circular needle when there are enough stitches to fit on the needle.

CROWN

Using MC, CO 8 sts. Distribute evenly among 4 dpns; place marker (pm) for beginning of rnd and join, being careful not to twist sts.

Shape Crown

RND 1: *K1-f/b; repeat from * to end—16 sts.

RND 2: *K2, pm; repeat from * to last 2 sts, k2—7 markers placed in addition to beginning of rnd marker.

INCREASE RND: Increase 8 sts this rnd, then every other rnd 25 times, as follows: *K1-f/b, knit to marker, slip marker (sm); repeat from * to end—224 sts.

finished measurements
28" head circumference, without elastic

yarn
Blue Sky Alpacas Alpaca Silk (50% alpaca/50% silk; 146 yards/50 grams): 2 hanks #120 White (MC)

Presencia Finca Perle Cotton size 8 (100% mercerized Egyptian cotton; 77 yards/10 grams): 1 ball #0007 Black (A)

needles
One 16" (40 cm) long circular (circ) needle size US 0 (2 mm)

One set of five double-pointed needles (dpn) size US 0 (2 mm)

Change needle size if necessary to obtain correct gauge.

notions
Stitch markers; crochet hook size US C/1 (2.25 mm); tapestry needle; 1 yard thin, round elastic cord; three glass jars; Jacquard acid dye in #637 Gun Metal, #639 Jet Black, and #638 Silver Grey; 1 bag fiberfill; plastic tarp or enough plastic bags to cover work area; 1 medium-sized craft paintbrush; small pot; white vinegar; metal tongs; clean towel or rag

gauge
32 sts and 52 rnds = 4" (10 cm) in Stockinette stitch (St st), using MC

Work even in St st until piece measures 3¾" from last increase or until Hat reaches top of brow, removing all 7 shaping markers on first rnd. BO all sts. Using crochet hook and MC, work 4 rnds sc (see tutorial on page 150) around BO edge. Thread CO tail onto tapestry needle and pull through 8 CO sts. Pull tightly and secure. Weave in all ends.

DYEING

Fill each jar with 1 cup hot water and ½ ounce dye—this yields a concentrated paint and more water can be added to make it thinner (and for a subsequently lighter shade) if needed. Wet Hat thoroughly with cool water and gently squeeze out excess water without wringing. Fill Hat with fiberfill and place on a work area protected with tarp or plastic bags.

Paint Hat

There is no set rule on how to do this. Have fun with it.

✳ *Customizing Tip:* When I applied the dye, I used the splotchy coloring of pigeon's wings as my inspiration. Beware that the colors will bleed slightly and run together like watercolor after you apply them. I rinsed the brush thoroughly before using the next color. You may cover all areas of the hat with paint, though I chose to maintain a few patches of the original cream color. ✳

When painting is complete, allow the Hat to dry. Fill small pot with ¼ cup vinegar and enough water to cover Hat. Bring solution to a near-boil and submerge Hat for approximately 15 minutes, being careful not to agitate it. Use tongs to carefully lift Hat out of the pot, let cool and rinse under cool water. Carefully press Hat in a clean towel or rag to remove excess water and lay flat to dry.

FINISHING

Decide what is to be the front of the Hat, then mark the center back. Using crochet hook and A, work 1 rnd sc around crocheted edge.

NEXT RND: Work 50 sc; holding elastic cord parallel to crocheted edge, work 100 sc over both edge and cord (see tutorial on page 155); drop cord and work sc to end. Pull ends of elastic cord to draw in back until piece fits as desired; secure cord with knot on either side, and weave ends into rnd of sc.

seaport skirt

During one of my first visits to New York many years ago, I watched fishmongers unload crates of fish at the South Street Seaport very early in the morning. The swirling cables in this skirt remind me of the overlapping tails in those crates and the vibrant activity of the workers on the dock. The stitch pattern makes the skirt hug in all the right places (and forgive in all the others), resulting in a fit that is flattering and comfortable.

WAISTBAND

CO 168 (192, 216, 240, 264, 288) sts. Place marker (pm) for beginning of rnd and join, being careful not to twist sts. Work even in St st until piece measures 1".

SKIRT

Begin Cable Pattern from Chart; work Rnds 1-66 once, working increases as indicated on Chart—224 (256, 288, 320, 352, 384) sts. Work Rnds 67-82 until piece measures 25¾ (26, 26¾, 27¼, 28, 28¼)". BO all sts.

FINISHING

With RS facing, using crochet hook, and holding elastic cord parallel to CO edge, work 1 rnd sc around CO edge and cord (see tutorial on page 155). Adjust elastic cord to desired measurements, secure with knot, and weave ends into rnd of sc. Work 2 rnds sc around BO edge. Weave in all ends. Block as desired.

sizes

X-Small (Small, Medium, Large, X-Large, 2X-Large)

finished measurements

34 ½ (39 ½, 44 ¼, 49 ¼, 54 ¼, 59)" hip

25 ¾ (26, 26 ¾, 27 ¼, 28, 28 ¼)" length

yarn

Karabella Aurora 8 (100% extrafine merino wool; 98 yards/50 grams): 10 (11, 13, 15, 17, 18) balls #20 Teal

needles

One 36" (90 cm) long or longer circular (circ) needle size US 8 (5 mm)

Change needle size if necessary to obtain correct gauge.

notions

Stitch marker; cable needle (cn); crochet hook size US E/4 (3.5 mm); 1 yard thin, round elastic cord

gauge

20 sts and 24 rnds = 4" (10 cm) in Stockinette stitch (St st)

26 sts and 24 rnds = 4" (10 cm) in Cable Pattern from Chart

CABLE PATTERN

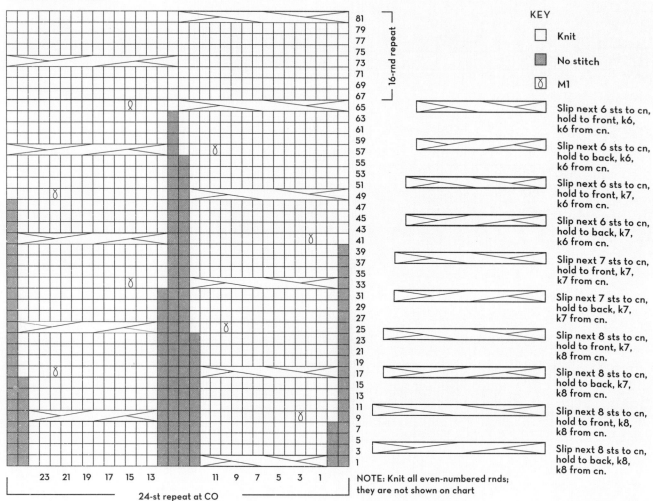

81
79
77
75
73
71
69
67
65
63
61
59
57
55
53
51
49
47
45
43
41
39
37
35
33
31
29
27
25
23
21
19
17
15
13
11
9
7
5
3
1

16-rnd repeat

23 21 19 17 15 13   11 9 7 5 3 1

24-st repeat at CO

KEY

☐ Knit

▧ No stitch

⧗ M1

Slip next 6 sts to cn, hold to front, k6, k6 from cn.

Slip next 6 sts to cn, hold to back, k6, k6 from cn.

Slip next 6 sts to cn, hold to front, k7, k6 from cn.

Slip next 6 sts to cn, hold to back, k7, k6 from cn.

Slip next 7 sts to cn, hold to front, k7, k7 from cn.

Slip next 7 sts to cn, hold to back, k7, k7 from cn.

Slip next 8 sts to cn, hold to front, k7, k8 from cn.

Slip next 8 sts to cn, hold to back, k7, k8 from cn.

Slip next 8 sts to cn, hold to front, k8, k8 from cn.

Slip next 8 sts to cn, hold to back, k8, k8 from cn.

NOTE: Knit all even-numbered rnds; they are not shown on chart

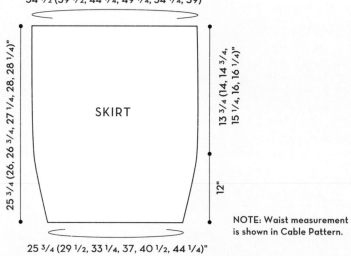

34 ½ (39 ½, 44 ¼, 49 ¼, 54 ¼, 59)"

SKIRT

25 ¾ (26, 26 ¾, 27 ¼, 28, 28 ¼)"

13 ¾ (14, 14 ¾, 15 ¼, 16, 16 ¼)"

12"

25 ¾ (29 ½, 33 ¼, 37, 40 ½, 44 ¼)"

NOTE: Waist measurement is shown in Cable Pattern.

wrap-it-up dress

A wrap dress is flattering when made from just about any material, but in fine knitted wool it becomes a sophisticated outfit for chilly days. The crocheted belt can be tied in any number of ways. For example, you can loop it once or twice around your waist, then tie it off in either a bow or a double knot.

STITCH PATTERNS

Woven Rib
(odd number of sts; 2-row repeat)
ROW 1 (RS): Purl.
ROW 2: K1, *slip 1 wyif, k1; repeat from * to end.
Repeat Rows 1 and 2 for Woven Rib.

Woven Rib in-the-Rnd
(even number of sts; 2-rnd repeat)
RND 1: Purl.
RND 2: *P1, slip 1 wyib; repeat from * to end.
Repeat Rnds 1 and 2 for Woven Rib in-the-Rnd

NOTES

✳ When working short rows in Woven Rib (for both the shoulders and the Sleeves) only the wraps worked on RS rows need to be hidden. When working WS rows, simply work the wrapped stitch, ignoring its wrap.

✳ After the initial Provisional CO, use Backward Loop CO for any other COs in this pattern (see Special Techniques, page 157).

sizes
X-Small (Small, Medium, Large, X-Large)

finished measurements
31½ (36, 40½, 44½, 49)" bust, closed

yarn
Shelridge Farm Soft Touch W4 (100% wool; 220 yards/100 grams): 13 (15, 17, 18, 20) hanks Olive

needles
One 40" (100 cm) long circular (circ) needle size US 7 (4.5 mm)

One 16" (40 cm) long circular needle size US 7 (4.5 mm)

One set of five double-pointed needles (dpn) size US 7 (4.5 mm)

Change needle size if necessary to obtain correct gauge.

notions
Waste yarn; stitch markers; removable stitch markers; crochet hook size US 7 (4.5 mm); 1¾ yards ½"-wide ribbon; sewing needle and matching thread

gauge
22 sts and 36 rows = 4" in Woven Rib

BACK

Using waste yarn, Provisional CO (see tutorial on page 16), and shorter circ needle, CO 75 (79, 83, 87, 91) sts. Working in Woven Rib and beginning with a RS row, work 1 row even.

NEXT ROW (WS): Work 20 (22, 23, 25, 26) sts, place marker (pm), work 35 (35, 37, 37, 39) sts, pm, work to end.

Shape Shoulders

ROWS 1 (RS) AND 2: Work to second marker, slip marker (sm), work 4 (5, 5, 6, 6) sts, wrp-t (see tutorial on page 19).

ROWS 3–8: Work to wrapped st from row before previous row, hide wrap, work 4 (5, 5, 5, 6) sts, wrp-t.

Work even, hiding remaining wraps as you come to them, until armholes measure 7 (7, 7¼, 7½, 7¾)" from end of shoulder shaping, ending with a WS row.

Shape Armholes

INCREASE ROW (RS): Increase 2 sts each side this row, then every other row 2 (4, 4, 5, 6) times, as follows, working new sts into pattern: K1-f/b, M1, work to last st, M1, k1-f/b—87 (99, 103, 111, 119) sts. Work 1 WS row even. Break yarn and set aside, leaving sts on needle for Body.

FRONT

With RS facing, carefully unravel Provisional CO and place first and last 20 (22, 23, 25, 26) sts on longer circ needle for Fronts. Leave center 35 (35, 37, 37, 39) sts on waste yarn for Back neck. Mark armhole edge for top of armhole.

Working BOTH SIDES AT THE SAME TIME using separate balls of yarn, working in Woven Rib and beginning with a RS row, work 2 rows even. Shape shoulders as for Back.

Work even until neck edge measures 5 (5, 5¼, 5½, 5¾)", ending with a RS row.

Shape Neck

Note: Neck and armhole shaping are worked at the same time; please read entire section through before beginning. Neck shaping will not be completed until after Back and Fronts are joined.

INCREASE ROW (WS): Increase 1 st each neck edge this row, every 4 rows 0 (1, 2, 3, 3) time(s), then every other row 35 (34, 34, 33, 34) times, as follows, working new sts into pattern: On Left Front, work to last st, M1, p1; on Right Front, p1, M1, work to end.

AT THE SAME TIME, when armholes measure same as for Back from marker to beginning of armhole shaping, shape armholes as for Back, ending with a WS row. Break yarn for Right Front.

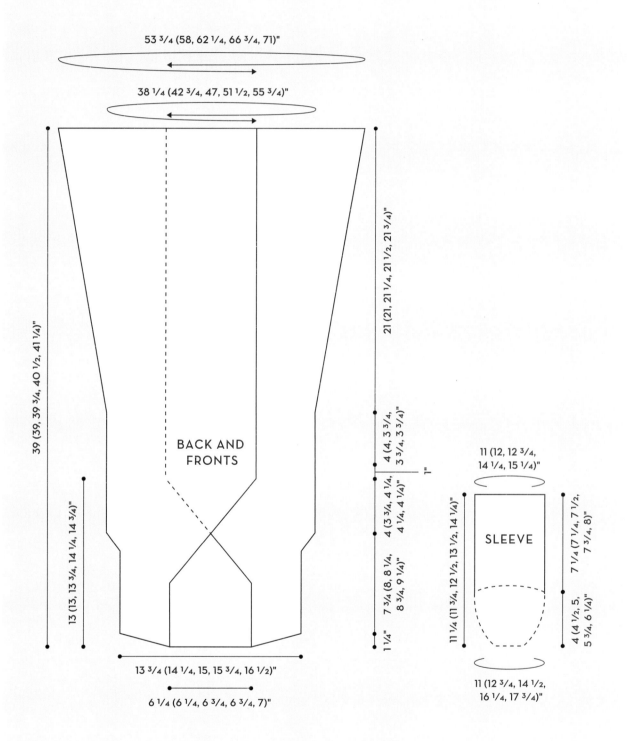

53 3/4 (58, 62 1/4, 66 3/4, 71)"

38 1/4 (42 3/4, 47, 51 1/2, 55 3/4)"

21 (21, 21 1/4, 21 1/2, 21 3/4)"

BACK AND FRONTS

39 (39, 39 3/4, 40 1/2, 41 1/4)"

13 (13, 13 3/4, 14 1/4, 14 3/4)"

4 (4, 3 3/4, 3 3/4, 3 3/4)"

4 (3 3/4, 4 1/4, 4 1/4, 4 1/4)"

1"

7 3/4 (8, 8 1/4, 8 3/4, 9 1/4)"

1 1/4"

13 3/4 (14 1/4, 15, 15 3/4, 16 1/2)"

6 1/4 (6 1/4, 6 3/4, 6 3/4, 7)"

11 (12, 12 3/4, 14 1/4, 15 1/4)"

SLEEVE

7 1/4 (7 1/4, 7 1/2, 7 3/4, 8)"

11 1/4 (11 3/4, 12 1/2, 13 1/2, 14 1/4)"

4 (4 1/2, 5, 5 3/4, 6 1/4)"

11 (12 3/4, 14 1/2, 16 1/4, 17 3/4)"

BODY

Join Back and Fronts

With RS facing, transfer Back sts, then Right Front sts to left-hand end of circ needle. Your sts should now be in the following order, from right to left, with RS facing: Left Front, Back, Right Front. Using yarn attached to Left Front, and continuing neck shaping as established, work across Left Front sts, CO 0 (0, 4, 6, 8) sts for underarm, pm for left side, CO 0 (0, 4, 6, 8) sts, work across Back sts, CO 0 (0, 4, 6, 8) sts for underarm, pm for right side, CO 0 (0, 4, 6, 8) sts, work across Right Front sts. Work even until neck shaping is complete, ending with a RS row—211 (235, 259, 283, 307) sts.

WORK BELT SLIT (WS): Work to first marker, join a second ball of yarn and work across remaining 149 (167, 185, 203, 221) sts. Work BOTH SIDES AT THE SAME TIME for 1", using separate balls of yarn, and ending with a WS row.

CLOSE SLIT (RS): Work across all sts with same ball of yarn.

Work even until piece measures 4 (4, 3¾, 3¾, 3¾)" from end of belt slit, ending with a WS row.

Shape Skirt

INCREASE ROW 1 (RS): Work 30 (32, 36, 40, 43) sts, (p1, k1, p1) into next st, work 29 (32, 36, 40, 43) sts, (p1, k1, p1) into next st, [work 29 (33, 36, 39, 43) sts, (p1, k1, p1) into next st] 4 times, work 30 (33, 37, 41, 43) sts—12 sts increased. Place a removable st marker in the center (knit) st of each 3-st increase group (6 markers placed). Work even for 25 rows.

INCREASE ROW 2 (RS): Increase in this manner, by working (p1, k1, p1) into each marked st, this rnd, every 26 rows 2 (2, 1, 0, 0) time(s), then every 28 rows 3 (3, 4, 5, 5) times, working new sts into pattern and moving marker up as you go—295 (319, 343, 367, 391) sts.

Work even until piece measures 30 (29¾, 30¼, 30½, 30¾)" from underarm. BO all sts.

SLEEVES

With RS facing, using shorter circ needle, and beginning at center of underarm, pick up and knit 60 (70, 80, 90, 98) sts evenly around armhole (see tutorial on page 22). Pm for beginning of rnd and join.

Shape Cap

ROW 1 (RS): Working in Woven Rib, work 40 (45, 50, 55, 59) sts, wrp-t.

ROW 2: Work 20 sts, wrp-t.

ROWS 3 AND 4: Work to wrapped st from row before previous row, hide wrap (on RS row only; ignore wrap on WS row), wrp-t.

Repeat Rows 3 and 4 sixteen (18, 21, 24, 26) times—3 (6, 8, 10, 12) sts remain unworked on either side of underarm marker. Change to Woven Rib in-the-Rnd. Work even until piece measures 7¼ (3¾, 2½, 1¼, 1¼)" from underarm, hiding remaining wrap as you come to it.

DECREASE RND: Decrease 2 sts this rnd, every (26, 10, 8, 8) rnds (1, 4, 1, 5) time(s), then every (0, 0, 10, 10) rnds (0, 0, 4, 1) time(s), as follows: P2tog, work to last 2 sts, ssp—(66, 70, 78, 84) sts.

Work even until piece measures (7¼, 7½, 7¾, 8)" from underarm.

All Sizes

BO all sts.

FINISHING

Collar

With RS facing, using longer circ needle and beginning at first neck increase, pick up and knit 24 (26, 28, 30, 32) sts up Right Front neck edge, 35 (35, 37, 37, 39) sts along Back neck, and 24 (26, 28, 30, 32) sts down Left Front neck edge—83 (87, 93, 97, 103) sts.

Note: Since Collar is meant to be folded over, the WS of the Collar faces the RS of the Dress.

INCREASE ROW (RS): Working in Woven Rib, increase 1 st each side this row, then every other row 13 times, as follows: P1, M1, work Woven Rib to last st, M1, p1—111 (115, 121, 125, 131). Work even if necessary until piece measures 3" from pick-up row. BO all sts. Using crochet hook, work 1 row sc (see tutorial on page 150) along BO edge.

Right Belt

Using crochet hook, ch 180 (196, 212, 228, 244). Work 3 rows sc. Fasten off. Sew to edge of Right Front, just below end of neck shaping.

Left Belt

Using crochet hook, ch 140 (156, 172, 188, 204). Work 3 rows sc. Fasten off. Sew to edge of Left Front, just below end of neck shaping.

Using crochet hook, work slip st around slit opening (see Special Techniques, page 157). Work 2 rows sc along bottom edge. Work 3 rnds sc around Sleeve cuffs.

Weave in all ends. Block as desired.

Cut 2 pieces of ribbon approximately 1" longer than center Front edges. Fold under ½" at either end and sew to WS edge of each Front (see tutorial on page 149).

I trimmed the inside edge of the dress with an olive silk ribbon, which is an elegant detail to see if the skirt opens slightly.

accordion cowl

After reading an article on Knitty.com about dyeing yarn with Kool-Aid, I was eager to try it. I chose natural white Morehouse Merino, a soft and fluffy yarn that soaks up the blitz-red of Tropical Punch Kool-Aid like a sponge. Once the yarn was dyed, I created a layered, accordion effect, using elastic cord for shaping, and then lined the top and bottom outside edges with thin, red velvet elastic trim.

PREPARE YARN

In a large bowl, soak a hank of yarn in hot water for 20 to 30 minutes. Fill large pot with water and heat to just below boiling. Add the Kool-Aid packets and stir until thoroughly dissolved. Remove yarn from bowl and gently squeeze out excess water. Add yarn to the dye bath. Ensure that the yarn is completely submerged in the dye solution, adding water to cover if necessary. Simmer for about 20 to 25 minutes, periodically turning the yarn over with tongs to help it evenly absorb the color. Turn off the heat when the water turns clear and allow the solution to cool until it can be handled comfortably. Rinse the yarn thoroughly in water the same temperature as the dye bath. Hang and allow to air dry. Wind yarn into balls.

COWL

CO 144 sts. Place marker (pm) for beginning of rnd and join, taking care not to twist sts. Work even until piece measures 2".

RUCHING RND: *BO all sts. With RS facing, using crochet hook, and holding elastic cord parallel to BO edge, work 1 rnd sc around BO edge and cord (see tutorial on page 155). Adjust elastic cord to desired measurements, secure with knot and weave ends into rnd of sc. Using circ needle, pick up and knit 144 sts from sc edge. Pm for beginning of rnd. Work even for 2"; repeat from * 5 times. Work even for 2". BO all sts.

Using crochet hook, work 3 rnds sc along top and bottom edges. Sew elastic velvet trim over the rnds of sc at both top and bottom (see tutorial on page 149). Weave in all ends.

finished measurements
24" circumference

yarn
Morehouse Merino 2-Ply Yarn (100% merino wool; 220 yards/2 ounces): 2 hanks Soft White

needles
One 24" (60 cm) long circular (circ) needle size US 5 (3.75 mm)

Change needle size if necessary to obtain correct gauge.

notions
Stitch marker; crochet hook size US F/5 (3.75 mm); 2½ yards thin, round elastic cord; 1 yard ¼"-wide elastic velvet trim; sewing needle and matching thread; ten 0.14-ounce packets Tropical Punch Kool-Aid unsweetened drink mix; large mixing bowl; large pot; metal tongs

gauge
24 sts and 32 rnds = 4" (10 cm) in Stockinette stitch (St st)

café tunic

Every now and then you find a yarn so lovely that you save it in your stash for just the right project. That's the reaction I had when I first discovered Blue Sky Alpaca's Worsted Hand Dyes, which is soft yet sturdy and perfect for capturing the casual, sweatshirt-type feeling of this tunic. I made the neckline wide, shaped the arm openings with elastic, and gathered the midriff with pleats, resulting in a comfortable, warm tunic that can be worn with just about anything.

NOTE

✳ If desired, the Skirt of the tunic can be worked from the bound-off edge of the Body, instead of sewing the pieces together at the end. To do this, after binding off at the end of the Body, work single crochet directly into the bound-off edge, skipping stitches for pleats as directed in Finishing. Work another round of single crochet, then pick up stitches onto circ needle and continue as instructed in Skirt.

BACK

Using waste yarn and Provisional CO (see tutorial on page 16), CO 98 (104, 112, 118, 124, 132) sts. Working in St st and beginning with a knit row, work 2 rows even.

NEXT ROW (RS): Knit 30 (32, 35, 36, 38, 41) sts, place marker (pm), work 38 (40, 42, 46, 48, 50) sts, pm, knit to end.

sizes
X-Small (Small, Medium, Large, X-Large, 2X-Large)

finished measurements
28-30 (32-34, 36-38, 40-42, 44-46, 48-50)" bust
34 (37 3/4, 41 1/2, 45 1/4, 49, 52 3/4)" hip

yarn
Blue Sky Alpacas Worsted Hand Dyes (50% alpaca/50% merino; 100 yards/100 grams): 10 (11, 12, 14, 15, 17) hanks #2015 Putty

needles
One 32" (80 cm) long circular (circ) needle size US 9 (5.5 mm)
Change needle size if necessary to obtain correct gauge.

notions
Waste yarn; stitch markers; crochet hook size US H/8 (5 mm); 1 yard thin, round elastic cord

gauge
17 sts and 23 rows = 4" (10 cm) in Stockinette stitch (St st)

Shape Shoulders

ROWS 1 (WS) AND 2: Work to second marker, slip marker (sm), work 3 (4, 5, 3, 4, 5) sts, wrp-t (see tutorial on page 19).

ROWS 3–14: Work to wrapped st from row before previous row, hide wrap, work 3 (3, 3, 4, 4, 4) sts, wrp-t—2 (3, 5, 2, 3, 5) sts remain unworked each side after last wrapped st.

Work even in St st, hiding remaining wraps as you come to them, until armholes measure 8 ¾ (9, 9 ½, 10, 10 ½, 10 ¾)" from end of shoulder shaping, ending with a RS row. Break yarn and transfer sts to waste yarn for Body.

FRONT

With RS facing, carefully unravel Provisional CO and place sts on circ needle for Front. Mark armhole edge for top of armhole.

NEXT ROW (RS): K30 (32, 35, 36, 38, 41) sts; join a second ball of yarn, BO 38 (40, 42, 46, 48, 50) sts, knit to end.

Working BOTH SIDES AT THE SAME TIME using separate balls of yarn, work 2 rnds even. Shape shoulders as for Back.

Work even in St st, hiding remaining wraps as you come to them, until neck edge measures 3 ¾ (3 ¾, 4 ¼, 4 ½, 4 ¾, 5 ¼)", ending with WS row. Break off second ball of yarn.

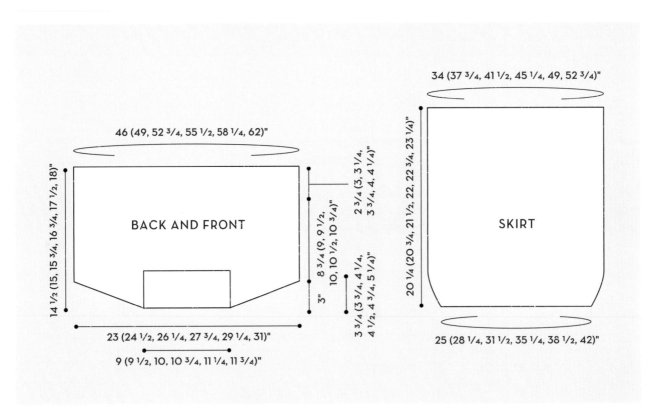

Join Fronts

NEXT ROW (RS): K30 (32, 35, 36, 38, 41) sts, CO 38 (40, 42, 46, 48, 50) sts, knit to end—98 (104, 112, 118, 124, 132) sts. Work even until armholes measure same as for Back from marker, ending with a WS row.

BODY

Join Back to Front

NEXT ROW (RS): Knit across Front sts, then across Back sts from waste yarn—196 (208, 224, 236, 248, 264) sts. Pm for beginning of rnd and join. Work even until piece measures 2¼ (3, 3¼, 3¾, 4, 4¼)" from join. BO all sts.

SKIRT

Ch 106 (120, 134, 150, 164, 178), join with slip st; work 1 rnd sc (see tutorial on page 150). Do not break yarn. Transfer st on crochet hook to circ needle, pick up and knit 105 (119, 133, 149, 163, 177) more sts along sc edge—106 (120, 134, 150, 164, 178). Pm for beginning of rnd. Work even in St st for 1", increase 14 (16, 18, 18, 20, 22) sts evenly spaced on first rnd—120 (136, 152, 168, 184, 200) sts.

Shape Skirt

NEXT RND: [K15 (17, 19, 21, 23, 25), pm] 7 times, knit to end.

INCREASE RND: Increase 8 sts this rnd, then every 6 rnds twice, as follows: *Knit to marker, M1; repeat from * to end—144 (160, 176, 192, 208, 224) sts. Work even until piece measures 20¼ (20¾, 21½, 22, 22¾, 23¼)" from pick-up edge. BO all sts.

FINISHING

Using crochet hook, work 1 rnd sc around neckline, working 1 sc in every st across Back neck, and 1 sc in every other row at neck edges. With RS facing, holding elastic cord parallel to edge, work 1 row sc around each arm opening, working cord into sc (see tutorial on page 155). Adjust elastic cords to desired measurements, secure with knots, and weave ends into sc. Work 1 rnd sc along bottom edge of skirt.

Sew Body's BO edge to Skirt's CO edge, creating 22 unattached pleats evenly spaced around waist, as follows: Work approximately 4-6 sts, then skip next 4 sts (which will remain unattached); continue in this manner around waist. Spacing between pleats should be even, though you may wish to add extra space between pleats under the arms.

Weave in all ends. Block as desired.

keffiyeh wrap

The stitch pattern for this wrap was inspired by the designs used for keffiyehs, traditional Arab headdresses in striking patterns made from thin, cotton cloth. My knitted version is made in luxurious baby alpaca yarn and is wide enough to wrap around your shoulders, though you can wear it as a thick scarf on an especially chilly day. Instead of tassels, which are used on traditional keffiyehs, I chose to line the edges with velvet trim for added texture and color.

NOTE

✳ Carry color not in use up right edge of work, making sure not to pull strand tightly when bringing color back into work.

STITCH PATTERNS

Knot Ridges I

(multiple of 2 sts + 3; 6-row repeat)

ROWS 1 AND 3 (RS): With MC, knit.

ROWS 2 AND 4: With MC, purl.

ROW 5: With A, k1, [k1, yo, k1] into next st, *slip 1, [k1, yo, k1] into next st; repeat from * to last st, k1.

ROW 6: With A, k1, k3tog-tbl, *slip 1, k3tog-tbl; repeat from * to last st, k1.

Repeat Rows 1–6 for Knot Ridges I.

finished measurements

Approximately 28 ½" wide × 40 ½" long, including edging

yarn

Misti Alpaca Suri & Silk (80% baby suri alpaca/20% silk; 109 yards/50 grams): 8 skeins each #VR1285 Jade (MC) and #AZ3743 Turquoise (A)

needles

One 32" (80 cm) long or longer circular (circ) needle size US 6 (4 mm)

Change needle size if necessary to obtain correct gauge.

notions

Waste yarn; 2 ½ yards ¼"-wide velvet trim to match A; crochet hook size US G/6 (4 mm); sewing needle and matching thread

gauge

23 sts and 38 rows = 4" (10 cm) in Knot Ridges I

Knot Ridges II
(multiple of 2 sts + 5; 8-row repeat)

ROW 1: (RS): With A, knit.

ROW 2: With A, purl.

ROW 3: With MC, k1, [k1, yo, k1] into next st, *slip 1, [k1, yo, k1] into next st; repeat from * to last st, k1.

ROW 4: With MC, k1, k3tog-tbl, *slip 1, k3tog-tbl; repeat from * to last st, k1.

ROWS 5 AND 6: Repeat Rows 1 and 2.

ROW 7: Using MC, k2, [k1, yo, k1] into next st, *slip 1, [k1, yo, k1] into next st; repeat from * to last 2 sts, k2.

ROW 8: Using MC, p2, k3tog-tbl, *slip 1, k3tog-tbl; repeat from * to last 2 sts, p2.

Repeat Rows 1–8 for Knot Ridges II.

WRAP

Using waste yarn and Provisional CO (see tutorial on page 16), CO 153 sts. Change to MC and knit 1 row.

Center Section
Work Rows 1–6 of Knot Ridges I 47 times, then Rows 1–4 once (piece measures approximately 30").

Top Border
Knit 2 rows A, 8 rows MC, 2 rows A, then 2 rows MC. Work Rows 1–8 of Knot Ridges II 4 times, then Rows 1–6 once. Knit 2 rows MC, 8 rows A, then 2 rows MC. BO all sts.

Bottom Border
Carefully unravel Provisional CO and place sts on circ needle. Knit 2 rows A, 8 rows MC, 2 rows A, then 2 rows MC. Work Rows 1–8 of Knot Ridges II 4 times, then Rows 1–6 once. Knit 2 rows MC, 8 rows A, then 2 rows MC. BO all sts.

FINISHING

Using crochet hook and MC, work 3 rows sc (see tutorial on page 150) along each side, working 1 sc in every other row. Weave in all ends. Block as desired. With RS facing, sew trim along each side edge to cover join between knit sts and crocheted edge (see tutorial on page 149).

ruffle cuff arm warmers

The inspiration for these ruffled arm warmers came from a beautiful window display of socks at a boutique in my neighborhood. I selected a colorful pair and used the top part of each sock for the arms. I then knit soft ruffles and attached them at the cuffs, covering the join with velvet trim.

RUFFLE STRIPS (make 6)

CO 147 sts.

ROW 1 (RS): P3, *k9, p3; repeat from * to end.

ROW 2 AND ALL WS ROWS: Knit the knit sts and purl the purl sts as they face you.

ROW 3: P3, *ssk, k5, k2tog, p3; repeat from * to end—123 sts remain.

ROW 5: P3, *ssk, k3, k2tog, p3; repeat from * to end—99 sts remain.

ROW 7: P3, *ssk, k1, k2tog, p3; repeat from * to end—75 sts remain.

ROW 9: P3, *slip 1 wyib, k2tog, psso, p3; repeat from * to end—51 sts remain.

Work even for 3 rows. BO all sts.

FINISHING

Cut foot off of each sock directly above heel. Fold cut edges ¼" to WS and sew in place. Sew trim over seam on inside of sock. Sew Strips together as follows: place first Strip RS down, then place second Strip on top of first strip, ½" above its top edge; sew in place with yarn. Repeat with third Strip, positioning it above second Strip and sewing into place. Repeat with remaining three Ruffle Strips to make two Cuffs.

With RS facing, lay top edge of first Cuff over outside top edge (edge with trim on WS) of sock. Make sure that Cuff reaches all the way around wrist; if more length is needed, work 1 to 3 rows sc along each side edge (see tutorial on page 150). Sew side edges together with needle and thread. Sew top edge of each Cuff to cut edge of each sock. Sew trim over join on RS.

yarn

Blue Sky Alpacas Alpaca Silk (50% alpaca/50% silk; 146 yards/50 grams): 2 hanks #100 Slate

needles

One 16" (40 cm) long circular (circ) needle size US 3 (3.25 mm)

Change needle size if necessary to obtain correct gauge.

notions

1 pair socks; 1 yard ½"-wide elastic velvet trim; sewing needle and matching thread; crochet hook size US D/3 (3.25 mm)

gauge

10 sts and 14 rows = 2" (5 cm) in Pattern

mulberry hat

Easy, cheerful, and elegant were the three words I had in mind when I designed this hat. A band of matching elastic trim sewn to the outside of the hat helps to accentuate the close fit at the top of the head and the slightly flared brim, while the rich, radiant mulberry yarn provides a blast of uplifting color—perfect for a gray and dreary day.

NOTE

✳ When starting the Hat, you may find it easier to work on 3 double-pointed needles (dpns) than on 4. Adjust stitch positions accordingly and change to 4 dpns when there are enough stitches to fit comfortably. Change to circular needle when there are enough stitches to fit on the needle.

CROWN

CO 8 sts. Distribute evenly among 4 dpns; place marker (pm) for beginning of rnd and join, being careful not to twist sts.

Shape Crown

RND 1: *K1-f/b; repeat from * to end—16 sts.

RND 2: *K2, pm; repeat from * to last 2 sts, k2—7 markers placed in addition to beginning of rnd marker.

INCREASE RND: Increase 8 sts this rnd, then every other rnd 14 (15, 16) times, as follows: *K1-f/b, knit to marker, slip marker (sm); repeat from * to end—136 (144, 152) sts.

Work even in St st until piece measures 2¼ (2½, 2¾)" from last increase, removing all 7 shaping markers on first rnd.

NEXT RND: *K17 (18, 19), pm; repeat from * 5 times, knit to end.

sizes
Small (Medium, Large)

finished measurements
17½ (19, 20¼)" head circumference

yarn
Debbie Bliss Cashmerino Aran (55% merino wool/33% microfibre/12% cashmere; 98 yards/50 grams): 2 (2, 3) balls #013 Wine

needles
One 16" (40 cm) long circular (circ) needle size US 6 (4 mm)

One set of five double-pointed needles (dpn) size US 6 (4 mm)

Change needle size if necessary to obtain correct gauge.

notions
Stitch markers; crochet hook size US E/4 (3.5 mm); tapestry needle; ¾ yard ½"-wide elastic ribbon; sewing needle and matching thread

gauge
22 sts and 26 rnds = 4" (10 cm) in Stockinette stitch (St st)

Shape Hat

DECREASE RND: Decrease 8 sts this rnd, then every rnd 4 times, as follows: *Knit to 2 sts before marker, k2tog; repeat from * to end—96 (104, 112) sts remain. BO all sts.

BRIM

Work 2 rnds sc (see tutorial on page 150) along BO edge. Using circ needle, pick up and knit 96 (104, 112) sts along crocheted edge. Pm for beginning of rnd and join.

INCREASE RND 1: *K1-f/b, k11 (12, 13); repeat from * to end—104 (112, 120) sts. Knit 1 rnd.

INCREASE RND 2: *K1-f/b, k12 (13, 14); repeat from * to end—112 (120, 128) sts. Knit 2 rnds. BO all sts. Using crochet hook, work 1 rnd sc around BO edge.

FINISHING

Thread CO tail onto tapestry needle and pull through 8 CO sts. Pull tightly and secure. Weave in all ends. Block as desired. Sew elastic ribbon to RS of hat, covering sc band entirely (see tutorial on page 149).

museum tunic

Thanks to its simple silhouette, this cowl-neck tunic easily transforms from casual to formal. Wear it over pants for an afternoon visit to a museum or pair it with boots for evening drinks with friends. Its versatility will make it a staple in your wardrobe for years to come. And worked on larger needles in Stockinette stitch, the knitting will fly by.

NOTE

✳ After the initial Provisional CO, use Backward Loop CO for any other COs in this pattern (see Special Techniques, page 157).

BACK

Using waste yarn, Provisional CO (see tutorial on page 16) and shorter circ needle, CO 46 (48, 50, 52, 54, 56, 58) sts. Working in St st and beginning with a knit row, work 2 rows even.

NEXT ROW (RS): K11 (12, 12, 13, 13, 14, 15), place marker (pm), k24 (24, 26, 26, 28, 28, 28), pm, knit to end.

Shape Shoulders

ROWS 1 (WS) AND 2: Work to second marker, slip marker (sm), work 3 (3, 3, 4, 4, 4, 5) sts, wrp-t (see tutorial on page 19).

ROWS 3 AND 4: Work to wrapped st from row before previous row, hide wrap, work 3 (3, 3, 3, 3, 4, 4) sts, wrp-t.

Work even, hiding remaining wraps as you come to them, until armholes measure 8" from end of shoulder shaping, ending with a WS row.

Shape Armholes

INCREASE ROW (RS): Increase 1 st each edge this row, then on every other row 0 (1, 2, 3, 4, 5, 6) time(s), as follows: K2, M1-R, knit to last 2 sts, M1, k2—48 (52, 56, 60, 64, 68, 72) sts. Work 1 WS row even. Break yarn, leaving sts on needle.

sizes

2X-Small (X-Small, Small, Medium, Large, X-Large, 2X-Large)

finished measurements

32 (34¾, 37¼, 40, 42¾, 45¼, 48)" bust

yarn

Debbie Bliss Cashmerino Superchunky (55% merino wool/ 33% microfibre/12% cashmere; 83 yards/100 grams): 9 (10, 11, 12, 13, 14, 15) skeins #19 Teal

needles

One 24" (60 cm) long circular (circ) needle size US 11 (8 mm)

One 32" (80 cm) long circular needle size US 11 (8 mm)

Change needle size if necessary to obtain correct gauge.

notions

Waste yarn; stitch markers; crochet hook size US H/8 (5 mm); 1½ yards ¾"-wide velvet trim; sewing needle and matching thread

gauge

12 sts and 18 rows = 4" (10 cm) in Stockinette stitch (St st)

FRONT

With RS facing, carefully unravel Provisional CO and place first and last 11 (12, 12, 13, 13, 14, 15) sts on longer circ needle. Leave center 24 (24, 26, 26, 28, 28, 28) sts on smaller circ needle for Back neck. Mark armhole edge for top of armhole.

Working BOTH SIDES AT THE SAME TIME using separate balls of yarn, work 2 rows even. Shape shoulders as for Back. Work even if necessary until neck edge measures 2 (2, 2¼, 2½, 2¾, 3, 3)", ending with a WS row.

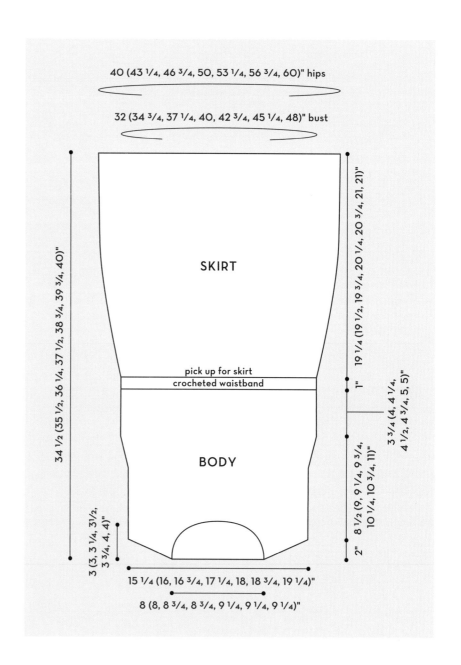

40 (43 ¼, 46 ¾, 50, 53 ¼, 56 ¾, 60)" hips

32 (34 ¾, 37 ¼, 40, 42 ¾, 45 ¼, 48)" bust

SKIRT

pick up for skirt
crocheted waistband

BODY

34 ½ (35 ½, 36 ¼, 37 ½, 38 ¾, 39 ¾, 40)"

19 ¼ (19 ½, 19 ¾, 20 ¼, 20 ¾, 21, 21)"

1"

3 ¾ (4, 4 ¼, 4 ½, 4 ¾, 5, 5)"

8 ½ (9, 9 ¼, 9 ¾, 10 ¼, 10 ¾, 11)"

2"

3 (3, 3 ¼, 3½, 3 ¾, 4, 4)"

15 ¼ (16, 16 ¾, 17 ¼, 18, 18 ¾, 19 ¼)"

8 (8, 8 ¾, 8 ¾, 9 ¼, 9 ¼, 9 ¼)"

NEXT ROW (RS): CO 3 sts at each neck edge twice—17 (18, 18, 19, 19, 20, 21) sts each side.

Join Fronts
NEXT ROW (RS): Knit across right Front sts, CO 12 (12, 14, 14, 16, 16, 16) sts for center neck, knit across left Front sts, breaking second ball of yarn—46 (48, 50, 52, 54, 56, 58) sts. Work even until armholes measure same as for Back from marker to beginning of armhole shaping, shape armholes as for Back, ending with a WS row—48 (52, 56, 60, 64, 68, 72) sts. Do not turn.

BODY

Join Back and Front
With RS facing, using yarn attached to Front, work across Back sts. Pm for beginning of rnd and join—96 (104, 112, 120, 128, 136, 144) sts. Work even until piece measures 3¾ (4, 4¼, 4½, 4¾, 5, 5)" from underarm. ✳ *Customizing Tip:* You may wish to transfer your sts to waste yarn and try the piece on at this point, before binding off, to ensure that the waistband falls where you want it. ✳ BO all sts.

WAISTBAND

Work 3 rnds sc (see tutorial on page 150) around BO edge of Body, working 1 sc in each BO st on first rnd, and 1 sc in each sc in following rnds. Fasten off. With RS facing, using shorter circ needle, pick up and knit 1 sc in each sc along crocheted edge—96 (104, 112, 120, 128, 136, 144) sts. Knit 8 rnds.

Shape Hip
INCREASE RND 1: *K7, k1-f/b; repeat from * to end—108 (117, 126, 135, 144, 153, 162) sts. Knit 8 rnds.

INCREASE RND 2: *K8, k1-f/b; repeat from * to end—120 (130, 140, 150, 160, 170, 180) sts. Work even until piece measures 19¼ (19½, 19¾, 20¼, 20¾, 21, 21)" from pick-up rnd. BO all sts.

FINISHING

Cowl
With RS facing, using shorter circ needle and beginning at right shoulder, knit across 24 (24, 26, 26, 28, 28, 28) Back neck sts from waste yarn, pick up and knit 12 (12, 14, 14, 16, 16, 16) sts along left Front neck edge, 24 (24, 26, 26, 28, 28, 28) sts from center Front neck sts, then 12 (12, 14, 14, 16, 16, 16) sts along right Front neck edge—72 (72, 80, 80, 88, 88, 88) sts. Pm for beginning of rnd and join. Work even in Rev St st for 5". *Note: Cowl will be folded over so that knit side will show.* BO all sts. Work 2 rnds sc along BO edge.

Work 2 rnds sc along bottom edge. Sew trim to WS of hem (see tutorial on page 149). Weave in all ends. Block as desired.

Velvet trim along the hem of this dress creates a luxurious effect.

cecily sweater

When working with an exquisitely soft yarn like baby alpaca, the less fuss, the better. For this sweater, I kept the design elements simple, and used elastic cord to shape the collar and sleeves. I named the sweater after my dear friend Cecily Parks, who, by example, has taught me a great deal about both elegance and the beauty of simplicity.

BACK

Using waste yarn and Provisional CO (see tutorial on page 16), CO 75 (80, 85, 90, 95, 100) sts. Working in St st and beginning with a RS row, work 2 rows even.

NEXT ROW (RS): K15 (17, 18, 20, 22, 24), place marker (pm), k45 (46, 49, 50, 51, 52), pm, knit to end.

Shape Shoulders

ROWS 1 (WS) AND 2: Work to second marker, slip marker (sm), work 5 (5, 6, 6, 7, 8) sts, wrp-t (see tutorial on page 19).

ROWS 3 AND 4: Work to wrapped st from row below previous row, hide wrap, work 4 (5, 5, 6, 7, 7) sts, wrp-t.

Work even in St st, hiding remaining wraps as you come to them, until armholes measure 7 ¼ (7 ¼, 7 ½, 7 ½, 7, 7)" from end of shoulder shaping, ending with WS row.

Shape Armholes

INCREASE ROW (RS): Increase 1 st each edge this row, then every other row 2 (4, 7, 9, 12, 14) times, as follows: K2, M1-R, knit to last 2 sts, M1, k2—81 (90, 101, 110, 121, 130) sts. Break yarn and transfer sts to waste yarn for Back.

FRONT

With RS facing, carefully unravel Provisional CO and place sts on circ needle for Front. Mark armhole edge for top of armhole.

sizes

X-Small (Small, Medium, Large, X-Large, 2X-Large)

finished measurements

30 ¾ (34 ¼, 38 ½, 42, 46, 49 ½)" bust

yarn

Misti Alpaca Baby Alpaca Royal (100% baby alpaca; 109 yards/50 grams): 7 (9, 10, 11, 13, 14) balls #9100 Lavender

needles

One 32" (80 cm) long circular (circ) needle size US 6 (4 mm)

Change needle size if necessary to obtain correct gauge.

notions

Waste yarn; stitch markers; crochet hook size US G/6 (4 mm); 2 ½ yards thin, round elastic cord; stitch markers

gauge

21 sts and 27 rows = 4" (10 cm) in Stockinette stitch (St st)

NEXT ROW (RS): K15 (17, 18, 20, 22, 24) sts; join a second ball of yarn, BO 45 (46, 49, 50, 51, 52) sts, knit to end.

Working BOTH SIDES AT THE SAME TIME using separate balls of yarn, work 2 rows even. Shape shoulders as for Back, ending with a WS row.

Shape Neck

INCREASE ROW (RS): Increase 1 st each neck edge this row, then every other row 7 (8, 9, 10, 10, 11) times, as follows: On right Front, work to last 2 sts, M1-R, k2; on left Front, k2, M1, work to end—23 (26, 28, 31, 33, 36) sts each side. Work 1 WS row even.

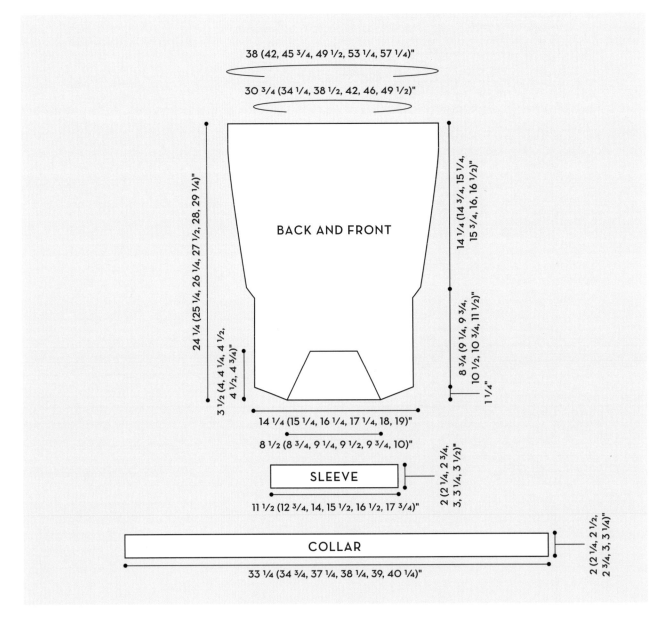

Join Fronts

NEXT ROW (RS): Work across right Front sts, CO 29 (28, 29, 28, 29, 28) sts
for center Front neck, work to end, breaking second ball of yarn. Work
even until armholes measure same as for Back from marker to beginning of
armhole shaping, shape armholes as for Back, ending with a WS row—81 (90,
101, 110, 121, 130) sts.

BODY

Join Back to Fronts

NEXT ROW (RS): Work across Front sts, then across Back sts from waste yarn—
162 (180, 202, 220, 242, 260) sts. Pm for beginning of rnd and join. Knit 3 rnds,
increasing 8 (10, 8, 10, 8, 10) sts evenly on last rnd—170 (190, 210, 230, 250, 270)
sts. Work even until piece measures 4 (4¼, 4½, 5, 5¼, 5½)" from underarm.

NEXT RND: *K17 (19, 21, 23, 25, 27), pm; repeat from * 9 times, knit to end.

Shape Body

INCREASE RND: Increase 10 sts this rnd, then every 12 rnds twice, as follows:
*Knit to marker, M1; repeat from * to end—200 (220, 240, 260, 280, 300)
sts. Work even until piece measures 14¼ (14¾, 15¼, 15¾, 16, 16½)" from
underarm. BO all sts.

SLEEVES (make 2)

CO 60 (67, 74, 81, 87, 93) sts. Working in St st, work even until piece measures
2 (2¼, 2¾, 3, 3¼, 3½)" in St st. BO all sts.

FINISHING

Using crochet hook, work 1 rnd sc (see tutorial on page 150) along neckline
and armholes, working 1 st in every st, or every 2 out of 3 rows. Work 3 rnds sc
along bottom edge.

Collar

CO 175 (182, 195, 201, 205, 211) sts. Pm for beginning of rnd and join, being
careful not to twist sts. Working in St st, work even for 2 (2¼, 2½, 2¾, 3,
3¼)". BO all sts. Work 2 rnds sc along BO edge. With RS facing, using crochet
hook and holding elastic cord parallel to crocheted edge, work 1 rnd sc around
crocheted edge and cord (see tutorial on page 155). Pull elastic ends and gather
Collar to match circumference of neckline; tie ends of cord in knot to secure.
Weave in ends of elastic through row of sc. Holding elastic cord parallel to CO
edge, work 1 rnd sc around CO edge and cord. Gather as for top edge and sew
to neckline, positioning beginning of rnd at center Back neck.

Sleeve Edging

Mark center of CO edge. Work 2 rows sc along BO edge. With RS facing, using
crochet hook and holding elastic cord parallel to crocheted edge, work 1 rnd sc
around each crocheted edge and cord. Pull elastic ends and gather Sleeve; tie in
knot to secure, and weave in ends of elastic through rnd of sc. Holding elastic
cord parallel to CO edge, work 1 row sc around each CO edge and cord. Gather
as for top edges. Sew Sleeves into armholes. Weave in all ends. Block as desired.

feather dress

This baby alpaca dress manages to be soft and light as a feather while also keeping you warm. The empire waist is drawn in and secured with a crocheted row of elastic cord and the low neckline invites all sorts of layering possibilities, from a pretty blouse to a simple T-shirt. Wear it as a short dress with tights or as a tunic over jeans—either way you'll brave the elements in style.

ABBREVIATION

M1-p-L (make 1 purlwise-left slanting): With the tip of the left-hand needle inserted from front to back, lift the strand between the 2 needles onto the left-hand needle; purl the strand through the back loop to increase 1 stitch.

BACK

Using shorter circ needle, waste yarn and Provisional CO (see tutorial on page 16), CO 58 (60, 64, 66, 70) sts. Working in St st and beginning with a knit row, work 1 row even.

NEXT ROW (WS): P11 (12, 13, 14, 15), place marker (pm), p36 (36, 38, 38, 40), pm, purl to end.

Shape Shoulders

ROWS 1 (RS) AND 2: Work to second marker, slip marker (sm), work 3 (4, 4, 4, 5) sts, wrp-t (see tutorial on page 19).

ROWS 3 AND 4: Work to wrapped st from row before previous row, hide wrap, work 3 (3, 3, 4, 4) sts, wrp-t.

Work even in St st, hiding remaining wraps as you come to them, until piece measures 7½" from end of shoulder shaping, ending with a WS row.

sizes
X-Small (Small, Medium, Large, X-Large)

finished measurements
35 ½ (38 ¾, 42 ¼, 45 ¾, 49 ¼)" bust

yarn
Misti Alpaca Chunky (100% baby alpaca; 108 yards/100 grams): 9 (10, 11, 12, 13) hanks #M718 Acorn Tan

needles
One 32" (80 cm) long circular (circ) needle size US 10 (6 mm)

One set of five double-pointed needles (dpn) size US 10 (6 mm)

One 16" (40 cm) long circular needle size US 10 (6 mm)

Change needle size if necessary to obtain correct gauge.

notions
Waste yarn; stitch markers; stitch holders; 3 yards thin, round elastic cord; ½ yard stretch ribbon; sewing needle and matching thread; crochet hook size US H/8 (5 mm)

gauge
14 sts and 20 rows = 4" (10 cm) in Stockinette stitch (St st)

INCREASE ROW (RS): Increase 1 st each side this row, then every other row 1 (3, 4, 6, 7) time(s), as follows: K2, M1-R, knit to last 2 sts, M1, k2—62 (68, 74, 80, 86) sts. Purl 1 WS row. Break yarn and set aside, leaving sts on needle.

FRONT

With RS facing, carefully unravel Provisional CO and place sts on longer circ needle for Front. Mark armhole edge for top of armhole.

NEXT ROW: K11 (12, 13, 14, 15); join a second ball of yarn, BO 36 (36, 38, 38, 40) sts, knit to end. Working BOTH SIDES AT THE SAME TIME using separate balls of yarn, knit 1 row. Shape shoulders as for Back.

Work even, hiding remaining wraps as you come to them, until neck edge measures 3¾ (4, 4, 4¼, 4¼)", ending with a WS row.

Shape Neck

Note: Neck and armhole shaping will be worked at the same time; please read entire section through before beginning.

INCREASE ROW (RS): Increase 1 st each neck edge this row, then every row 17 (17, 18, 18, 19) times, as follows: RS rows: On right Front, knit to last 2 sts, M1-R, k2; on left Front, k2, M1, knit to end. WS rows: On left Front, purl to last 2 sts, M1-p-L, p2; on right Front, p2, M1-P, purl to end. AT THE SAME TIME, when armholes measure same as for Back from marker to beginning of armhole shaping, shape armholes as for Back.

Join Fronts

NEXT ROW (RS): Continuing with armhole shaping, work across right Front sts, then left Front sts, breaking second ball of yarn. Continue until neck and armhole shaping are complete, ending with a WS row—62 (68, 74, 80, 86) sts.

BODY

Join Back and Front

NEXT ROW (RS): Work across Front sts, then across Back sts—124 (136, 148, 160, 172) sts. Pm for beginning of rnd and join. Work even in St st for ¾ (1, 1½, 1½, 2)". ✳ *Customizing Tip:* You may wish to transfer your stitches to waste yarn and try the piece on at this point, before binding off. The piece should sit comfortably below your bustline. Work additional rows if necessary to ensure proper fit. ✳ BO all sts.

WAISTBAND

With RS facing, using crochet hook and holding elastic cord parallel to BO edge, work 1 rnd sc around BO edge and cord, working 1 sc in each BO st (see tutorial on page 155). Adjust elastic cord to desired measurements, secure with knot and weave ends into row of sc.

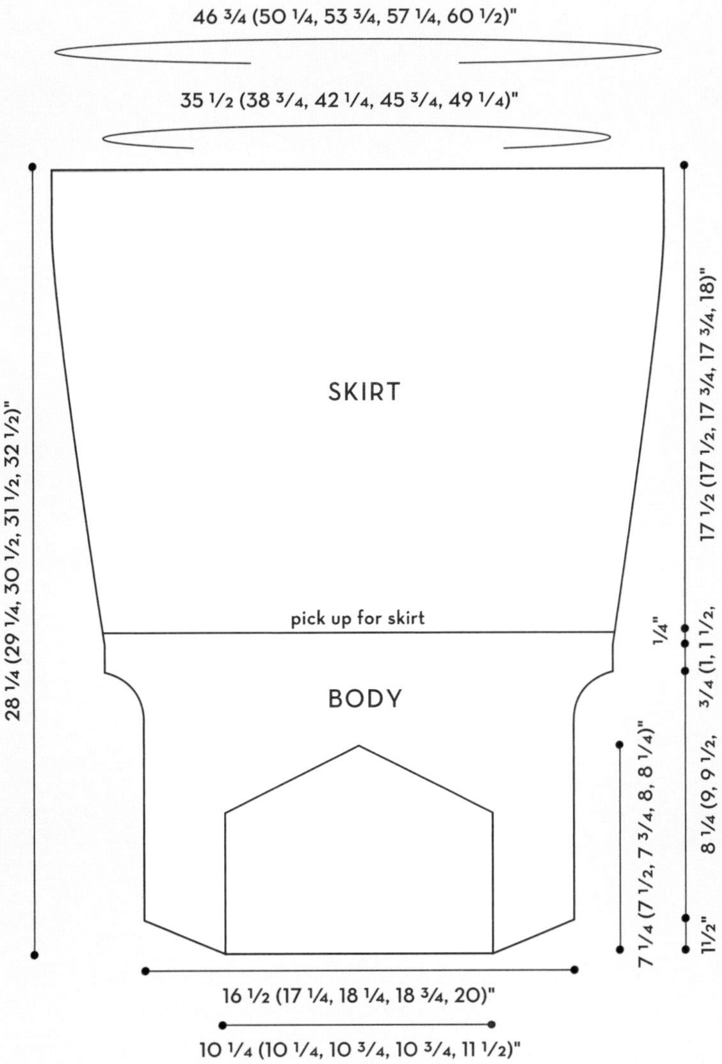
46 3/4 (50 1/4, 53 3/4, 57 1/4, 60 1/2)"
35 1/2 (38 3/4, 42 1/4, 45 3/4, 49 1/4)"
SKIRT
pick up for skirt
BODY
28 1/4 (29 1/4, 30 1/2, 31 1/2, 32 1/2)"
17 1/2 (17 1/2, 17 3/4, 17 3/4, 18)"
1/4"
3/4 (1, 1 1/2, 1 1/2, 2)"
8 1/4 (9, 9 1/2, 10 1/2, 10 3/4)"
1 1/2"
7 1/4 (7 1/2, 7 3/4, 8, 8 1/4)"
16 1/2 (17 1/4, 18 1/4, 18 3/4, 20)"
10 1/4 (10 1/4, 10 3/4, 10 3/4, 11 1/2)"

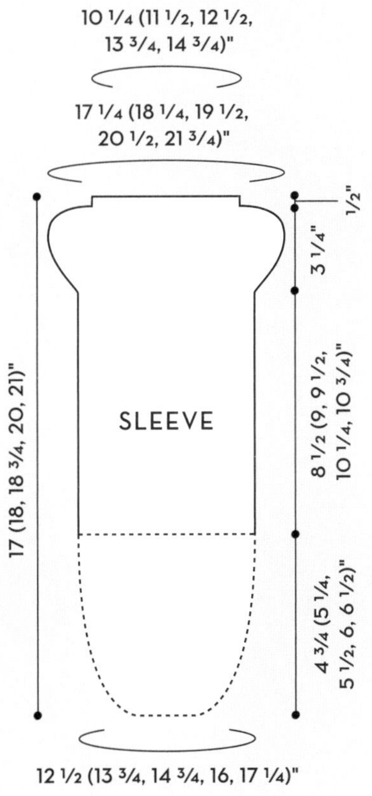
10 1/4 (11 1/2, 12 1/2, 13 3/4, 14 3/4)"
17 1/4 (18 1/4, 19 1/2, 20 1/2, 21 3/4)"
SLEEVE
17 (18, 18 3/4, 20, 21)"
1/2"
3 1/4"
8 1/2 (9, 9 1/2, 10 1/4, 10 3/4)"
4 3/4 (5 1/4, 5 1/2, 6, 6 1/2)"
12 1/2 (13 3/4, 14 3/4, 16, 17 1/4)"

The double crochet border makes a great foundation on which to sew stretch ribbon trim.

SKIRT

Using longer circ needle, pick up and knit 1 st in each sc in Waistband—124 (136, 148, 160, 172) sts. Pm for beginning of rnd and join. Knit 5 rnds.

Shape Skirt

NEXT RND: [K15 (17, 18, 20, 21), pm, k16 (17, 19, 20, 22), pm] 4 times, omitting final pm.

INCREASE RND: Increase 8 sts this rnd, then every 5 rnds 4 times, as follows: *M1, knit to next marker, slip marker (sm); repeat from * to end—164 (176, 188, 200, 212) sts. Work even until piece measures 17½ (17½, 17¾, 17¾, 18)" from pick-up rnd. BO all sts.

SLEEVES

With RS facing, using shorter circ needle and beginning at center of underarm, pick up and knit 44 (48, 52, 56, 60) sts evenly around armhole (see tutorial on page 22). Pm for beginning of rnd and join.

Shape Cap

ROW 1: K30 (32, 34, 36, 38), wrp-t.

ROW 2: P16, wrp-t.

ROWS 3-24 (26, 28, 30, 32): Work to wrapped st from row before previous row, hide wrap, wrp-t—3 (4, 5, 6, 7) sts remain unworked on either side of underarm marker. Work even until piece measures 8½ (9, 9½, 10¼, 10¾)" from underarm, hiding remaining wrap as you come to it.

Shape Sleeve

Note: Change to dpns when necessary for number of sts on needles.

NEXT RND: [K11 (12, 13, 14, 15), pm] 4 times, omitting final pm.

INCREASE RND: Increase 4 sts this rnd, then every 5 rnds 3 times, as follows: *Knit to marker, M1, sm; repeat from * to end of rnd—60 (64, 68, 72, 76) sts. Remove all 3 shaping markers.

Shape Cuff

DECREASE RND 1: [K2tog, k5 (6, 6, 7, 7), pm, k2tog, k6 (6, 7, 7, 8), pm] 4 times, omitting final pm—52 (56, 60, 64, 68) sts remain.

DECREASE RND 2: Decrease 8 sts this rnd, then every rnd once, as follows: [K2tog, knit to marker] 8 times—36 (40, 44, 48, 52) sts remain. BO all sts.

FINISHING

Work 1 rnd sc, working 1 sc in every other st around neckline and in every st across Back neck. Work 1 rnd dc (see tutorial on page 152) around sleeve cuffs and along bottom edge. Weave in all ends. Block as desired. Sew trim along inside of bottom edge (see tutorial on page 149).

annie hat

I channeled Woody Allen's Annie Hall for this hat, and crocheted pipe cleaners into the brim to help hold its iconic shape. With over 120 colors of Tahki's Cotton Classic yarn available, picking a shade for this hat is not unlike choosing a crayon from an enormous box.

NOTES

※ When starting the Hat, you may find it easier to work on 3 double-pointed needles (dpns) than on 4. Adjust stitch positions accordingly and change to 4 dpns when there are enough stitches to fit comfortably. Change to circular needle when there are enough stitches to fit on the needle.

※ Brim is shaped by working rounds of single crochet over linked pipe cleaners and bound-off edge. Link pipe cleaners by overlapping ends by about 1" and twisting firmly. Press together and smooth the join, trimming any sharp ends with scissors. Link 7 pipe cleaners together for first section and 8 for second section.

CROWN

CO 8 sts. Distribute evenly on among 4 dpns; place marker (pm) for beginning of rnd and join, being careful not to twist sts.

Shape Crown

RND 1: *K1-f/b; repeat from * to end—16 sts.

RND 2: *K2, pm; repeat from * to last 2 sts, k2—7 markers placed in addition to beginning of rnd marker.

INCREASE RND: Increase 8 sts this rnd, then every other rnd 11 (12, 13) times, as follows: *K1-f/b, knit to marker, slip marker (sm); repeat from * to end—112 (120, 128) sts.

Work even in St st until piece measures 2½ (2¾, 3)" from last increase, or until Hat fits comfortably just above your ears. BO all sts. Using crochet hook, work 3 rnds sc (see tutorial on page 150) around BO edge, working 1 sc in each BO st on first rnd, then 1 sc in each sc on following rnds.

sizes

Small (Medium, Large)

finished measurements

18 ¾ (20, 21 ¼)" head circumference

yarn

Tahki Yarns Cotton Classic (100% mercerized cotton; 108 yards/50 grams): 4 hanks #3248 Milk Chocolate

needles

One set of five double-pointed needles (dpn) size US 5 (3.75 mm)

One 16" (40 cm) long circular (circ) needle size US 4 (3.5 mm)

One 24" (60 cm) long circular needle size US 4 (3.5 mm)

notions

Stitch markers; crochet hook size US E/4 (3.5 mm); tapestry needle; approximately fifteen 12"-long pipe cleaners in coordinating color; 3 yards ¼"-wide trim; sewing needle and matching thread

gauge

24 sts and 30 rnds = 4" (10 cm) in Stockinette stitch (St st)

FIRST BRIM SECTION

Using longer circ needle, pick up and knit 1 st in each sc around BO edge—112 (120, 128) sts. Pm for beginning of rnd and join. Knit 1 rnd.

INCREASE RND: *K4, M1; repeat from * to end—140 (150, 160) sts. Work in St st for 1". BO all sts.

With RS facing, using crochet hook and holding linked pipe cleaners parallel to CO edge, work 3 rnds of sc as for Crown, around BO edge and pipe cleaners. *Note: You may refer to elastic cord tutorial on page 155 as the pipe cleaners are attached to the BO edge using the same method.*

SECOND BRIM SECTION

Pick up and knit 140 (150, 160) sts evenly around BO edge. Pm for beginning of rnd. Knit 1 rnd.

NEXT (INCREASE) RND: *K5, M1; repeat from * to end—168 (180, 192) sts. Work in St st for 1". BO all sts.

With RS facing, using crochet hook and holding linked pipe cleaners parallel to CO edge, work 3 rnds sc as for Crown, around BO edge and pipe cleaners.

FINISHING

Thread CO tail onto tapestry needle and pull through 8 CO sts. Pull tightly and secure. Weave in all ends. Shape Brim, pulling outward to ensure pipe cleaners are taut. Sew trim neatly over bands of sc on both sides of Hat (see tutorial on page 149).

daytona belt

I found this wide, colorful trim at Daytona Trimming in New York City and immediately envisioned it as a lining for a belt. I picked a smooth cotton yarn for the belt's exterior and calculated how many stitches would be needed to match the trim's width. I then sewed the trim to the knitted strap and attached a wooden buckle.

ABBREVIATION

RT: K2tog, but do not drop sts from left-hand needle. Insert right-hand needle between 2 sts just worked and knit first st again; slip both sts from left-hand needle together.

STITCH PATTERN

Twist Field Pattern

(multiple of 3 sts; 4-row repeat)

ROW 1: *RT, k1; repeat from * to end of row.

ROWS 2 AND 4: Purl

ROW 3: *K1, RT; repeat from * to end of row.

Repeat Rows 1-4 for Twist Field Pattern.

BELT

CO 12 sts. Work Rows 1-4 of Twist Field Pattern until piece measures 44", or to desired length. BO all sts.

FINISHING

Weave in all ends and block piece. Cut felt into five 2"-wide strips. Sew strips together end to end, then trim to form a 44"-long strip. With WS of Belt facing up, lay felt strip, then trim on Belt, and sew through all edges on all sides, tucking corners in at one end to round out tip. Insert opposite square end through buckle, fold down 2" and sew securely to WS of Belt.

finished measurements
2" wide x 42" long

yarn
Tahki Yarns Cotton Classic (100% mercerized cotton; 108 yards/50 grams): 1 hank #3336 Bittersweet Chocolate

needles
One pair straight needles size US 6 (4 mm)

notions
Sewing needle and heavyweight matching thread; two 8 x 10" pieces craft felt; 1 ½ yards 2"-wide ribbon trim; one 2"-diameter belt buckle

gauge
12 sts and 15 rows = 2" (5 cm) in Twist Field Pattern

blueberry cardigan

The graceful sleeves for this cardigan accentuate the yarn's luxurious, weighty nature and are worked differently than the sleeves on the other garments in this book. They are a version of the kimono sleeve template from *Knitting from the Top*, where sleeve stitches are cast on at the same time as body stitches and are worked top-down in one piece. A row of small eyehooks sewn down the front helps keep the opening uncluttered and smooth.

STITCH PATTERNS

Puff Rib I
(multiple of 3 sts + 2; 4-row repeat)
ROW 1 (RS): P2, *yo, k1, yo, p2; repeat from * to end—2 sts increased each repeat.
ROW 2: K2, *p3, k2; repeat from * to end.
ROW 3: P2, *k3, p2; repeat from * to end.
ROW 4: K2, *p3tog, k2; repeat from * to end (original st count restored).
Repeat Rows 1-4 for Puff Rib I.

Puff Rib II
(multiple of 4 sts + 3; 4-row repeat)
ROW 1 (RS): P3, *yo, k1, yo, p3; repeat from * to end—2 sts increased each repeat.
ROW 2: K3, *p3, k3; repeat from * to end.
ROW 3: P3, *k3, p3; repeat from * to end.
ROW 4: K3, *p3tog, k3; repeat from * to end (original st count restored).
Repeat Rows 1-4 for Puff Rib II.

sizes
X-Small (Small, Medium, Large, X-Large, 2X-Large)

finished measurements
32 (36 1/2, 40 3/4, 45 1/4, 49 1/2, 53 3/4)" bust, including Front bands

yarn
Blue Sky Alpacas Alpaca Silk (50% alpaca/50% silk; 146 yards/50 grams): 13 (15, 19, 21, 25, 30) hanks #140 Blueberry

needles
Two 40" (100 cm) long or longer circular (circ) needles size US 10 (6 mm)
Change needle size if necessary to obtain correct gauge.

notions
Waste yarn; stitch markers; crochet hook size US E/4 (3.5 mm); 20 size-0 hooks and eyes in black; sewing needle and matching thread; 1 1/2 to 2 1/2 yards 1/2"-wide sheer navy ribbon

gauge
11 sts and 18 rows = 4" (10 cm) in Puff Rib I, using 2 strands of yarn held together

Puff Rib III

(multiple of 5 sts + 4; 4-row repeat)

ROW 1 (RS): P4, *yo, k1, yo, p4; repeat from * to end—2 sts increased each repeat.

ROW 2: K4, *p3, k4; repeat from * to end.

ROW 3: P4, *k3, p4; repeat from * to end.

ROW 4: K4, *p3tog, k4; repeat from * to end (original st count restored).

Repeat Rows 1–4 for Puff Rib III.

NOTE

✳ After the initial Provisional CO, use Backward Loop CO for any other COs in this pattern (see Special Techniques, page 157).

BACK/SLEEVES

Using waste yarn and Provisional CO (see tutorial on page 16), CO 104 (110, 122, 128, 140, 152) sts. With 2 strands of yarn held together, work 8 (9, 10 ¾, 11 ½, 13 ¼, 15)" in Puff Rib I, ending with Row 4 of Puff Rib I. Break yarn and transfer first and last 30 (30, 33, 33, 36, 39) sts to waste yarn for Sleeves; transfer remaining 44 (50, 56, 62, 68, 74) sts to separate waste yarn for Body.

FRONT/SLEEVES

With RS facing, carefully unravel Provisional CO and place sts on circ needle for Front. Mark Sleeve edge for top of Sleeve. Place marker (pm) 38 (41, 47, 47, 53, 59) sts in from each edge.

NEXT ROW (RS): Using 2 strands of yarn held together, beginning with Row 1 of Puff Rib I, work to marker; join a second ball of yarn, BO 28 (28, 28, 34, 34, 34) sts for Back neck, work to end. Working BOTH SIDES AT THE SAME TIME using separate balls of yarn, work even in Puff Rib I until neck edge measures 2 ½ (3 ¼, 3 ¼, 3 ¼, 4 ¼, 4 ¼)", ending with Row 3 of Puff Rib I.

Shape Neck

NEXT ROW (RS): On Right Front, work to end, CO 12 (12, 12, 15, 15, 15) sts; on Left Front, CO 12 (12, 12, 15, 15, 15) sts, work to end—50 (53, 59, 62, 68, 74) sts each side. Work even until piece measures 8 (9, 10 ¾, 11 ½, 13 ¼, 15)" from marker, ending with Row 4 of Puff Rib I. Transfer first and last 30 (30, 33, 33, 36, 39) sts to waste yarn for Sleeves. Leave remaining sts on the needle for Body.

BODY

Join Back and Fronts

With RS facing, transfer center 44 (50, 56, 62, 68, 74) Back sts, then Right Front sts to left-hand end of circ needle. Your sts should now be in the following order, from right to left, with RS facing: Left Front, center Back, Right Front—84 (96, 108, 120, 132, 144) sts.

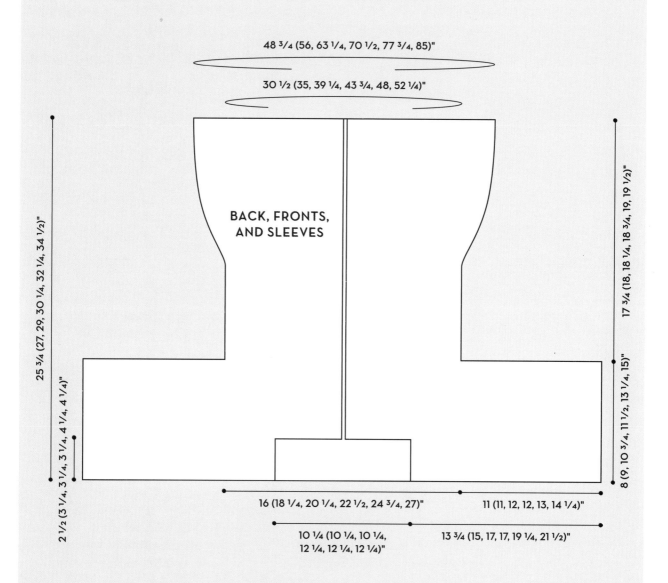

48 ¾ (56, 63 ¼, 70 ½, 77 ¾, 85)"

30 ½ (35, 39 ¼, 43 ¾, 48, 52 ¼)"

BACK, FRONTS,
AND SLEEVES

25 ¾ (27, 29, 30 ¼, 32 ¼, 34 ½)"

17 ¾ (18, 18 ¼, 18 ¾, 19, 19 ½)"

8 (9, 10 ¾, 11 ½, 13 ¼, 15)"

2 ½ (3 ¼, 3 ¼, 3 ¼, 4 ¼, 4 ¼)"

16 (18 ¼, 20 ¼, 22 ½, 24 ¾, 27)"

11 (11, 12, 12, 13, 14 ¼)"

10 ¼ (10 ¼, 10 ¼, 12 ¼, 12 ¼, 12 ¼)"

13 ¾ (15, 17, 17, 19 ¼, 21 ½)"

NEXT ROW (RS): Work to last 2 Left Front sts, [p2tog] twice, work to last 2 Back sts, [p2tog] twice, work to end—80 (92, 104, 116, 128, 140) sts remain. Work even until piece measures 7" from underarm, ending with Row 3 of Puff Rib I Pattern.

INCREASE ROW 1 (WS): K1, M1, k1, *p3tog, k1, M1, k1; repeat from * to end— 107 (123, 139, 155, 171, 187) sts. Change to Puff Rib II. Work even until piece measures 13" from underarm, ending with Row 3 of Puff Rib II.

INCREASE ROW 2 (WS): K2, M1, k1, *p3tog, k2, M1, k1; repeat from * to end—134 (154, 174, 194, 214, 234) sts. Change to Puff Rib III. Work even until piece measures 17¼ (18, 18¼, 18¾, 19, 19½)", or to desired length from underarm. BO all sts.

FINISHING

With WS facing, join Sleeves along lower edge using 3-needle BO method, as follows: Place sts to be joined onto 2 same-sized needles; hold pieces to be joined with RSs facing each other and needles parallel, both pointing to the right. Holding both needles in your left hand, using working yarn and a third needle the same size or 1 size larger, insert third needle into first st on front needle, then into first st on back needle; knit these 2 sts together; *knit next st from each needle together (2 sts on right-hand needle); pass first st over second st to BO 1 st. Repeat from * until 1 st remains on third needle; cut yarn and fasten off.

Sleeve Edging

RND 1: With RS facing, using crochet hook, work 48 (54, 64, 70, 80, 90) sc around Sleeve opening (see tutorial on page 150), slip st to beginning of rnd (see Special Techniques, page 157).

RND 2: *Sc, skip next st; repeat from * to end—24 (27, 32, 35, 40, 45) sts remain. Work 2 rnds dc (see tutorial on page 152).

Work 1 row sc along neck opening and 3 rows along each Front edge. Sew hooks and eyes to Front bands. Sew trim to WS of bottom edge (see tutorial on page 149). Weave in all ends. Block as desired.

coney sweater

The color palette for this sweater came from an old postcard I bought at a secondhand store years ago, featuring the Cyclone roller coaster at Coney Island. I tried to capture a bit of the amusement park's theatricality here with vivid colors and voluminous sleeves, which I flared near the wrist and gathered dramatically at the cuff. For extra polish, I lined the inside hem with cream-colored velvet trim.

STITCH PATTERNS

Body Stripe Pattern
(92-rnd panel)
Working in St st, work 3 rnds A, 9 rnds MC, 6 rnds B, 3 rnds C, 2 rnds D, 13 rnds C, 2 rnds E, 6 rnds F, 2 rnds A, 6 rnds B, 2 rnds A, 13 rnds B, 2 rnds A, 6 rnds F, 2 rnds E, 6 rnds C, and 9 rnds D.

Sleeve Stripe Pattern
(25-rnd panel)
Working in St st, work 2 rnds A, 5 rnds B, 2 rnds E, 7 rnds D, 7 rnds C, and 2 rnds F.

NOTES

✳ After the initial Provisional CO, use Backward Loop CO for any other COs in this pattern (see Special Techniques, page 157).

✳ In order to avoid a shift in stitches when working stripes in the round, you can employ a jogless color change, as follows: Work one round with the new color, remove beginning of the round marker, lift the previous-color stitch below the next new-color stitch onto the left-hand needle; k2tog (lifted stitch of previous-color and first stitch of new color), replace the marker. The beginning of the round will move 1 stitch to the left at each color change.

sizes
X-Small (Small, Medium, Large, X-Large)

finished measurements
33 1/2 (37 1/2, 41 3/4, 46, 50)" bust

yarn
Louet Gems Light Worsted Weight (100% merino wool; 175 yards/100 grams): 6 (7, 8, 9, 10) hanks #30 Cream (MC); 1 hank each #01 Champagne (A), #50 Sage (B), #47 Terra Cotta (C), #05 Goldilocks (D), #58 Burgundy (E), and #26 Crabapple (F)

needles
One 32" (80 cm) long circular (circ) needle size US 5 (3.75 mm)

One 16" (40 cm) long circular needle size US 5 (3.75 mm)

One set of five double-pointed needles (dpn) size US 5 (3.75 mm) for sizes X-Small, Small, and Medium

Change needle size if necessary to obtain correct gauge.

notions
Waste yarn; stitch markers; crochet hook size US H/8 (5 mm); 1 yard thin, round elastic cord; 1 1/2 yards 3/4"-wide velvet ribbon; sewing needle and matching thread

gauge
23 sts and 31 rows = 4" (10 cm) in Stockinette stitch (St st)

BACK

Using waste yarn, Provisional CO (see tutorial on page 16), and shorter circ needle, CO 90 (96, 102, 108, 114) sts. Change to MC. Working in St st and beginning with a RS row, work 2 rows even.

NEXT ROW (RS): K24 (25, 26, 27, 28), place marker (pm), k42 (46, 50, 54, 58), pm, knit to end.

Shape Shoulders

ROWS 1 (WS) AND 2: Purl to second marker, slip marker (sm), work 3 (4, 4, 5, 3) sts, wrp-t (see tutorial on page 19).

ROWS 3–10: Work to wrapped st from row before previous row, hide wrap, work 3 (3, 3, 3, 4) sts, wrp-t.

Work even, hiding remaining wraps as you come to them, until armholes measure 7¾ (8, 8¼, 8½, 8¾)" from end of shoulder shaping, ending with a WS row.

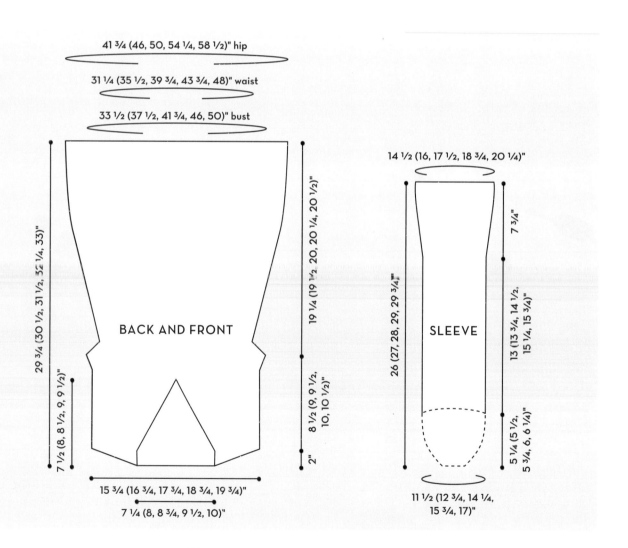

41¾ (46, 50, 54¼, 58½)" hip

31¼ (35½, 39¾, 43¾, 48)" waist

33½ (37½, 41¾, 46, 50)" bust

14½ (16, 17½, 18¾, 20¼)"

29¾ (30½, 31½, 32¼, 33)"

19¼ (19½, 20, 20¼, 20½)"

7¾"

BACK AND FRONT

SLEEVE

26 (27, 28, 29, 29¾)"

13 (13¾, 14½, 15¼, 15¾)"

7½ (8, 8½, 9, 9½)"

8½ (9, 9½, 10, 10½)"

2"

5¼ (5½, 5¾, 6, 6¼)"

15¾ (16¾, 17¾, 18¾, 19¾)"

7¼ (8, 8¾, 9½, 10)"

11½ (12¾, 14¼, 15¾, 17)"

Shape Armholes

INCREASE ROW (RS): Increase 1 st each edge this row, then every other row 2 (3, 4, 5, 6) times, as follows: K2, M1-R, knit to last 2 sts, M1, k2—96 (104, 112, 120, 128) sts. Purl 1 WS row. Break yarn, leaving sts on needle for Body.

FRONT

With RS facing, carefully unravel Provisional CO and place sts on longer circ needle for Front. Mark armhole edge for top of armhole.

NEXT ROW (RS): K24 (25, 26, 27, 28); join a second ball of yarn, BO 42 (46, 50, 54, 58) sts, knit to end. WORKING BOTH SIDES AT THE SAME TIME using separate balls of yarn, work 3 rows in St st, beginning with a knit row. Shape shoulders as for Back. Work even until neck edge measures 2", ending with a WS row.

Shape Neck

Note: For some of the sizes, neck and armhole shaping will be worked at the same time; please read entire section through before beginning.

INCREASE ROW (RS): Increase 1 st each neck edge this row, then every other row 20 (22, 24, 26, 28) times, as follows: On right Front, knit to last 2 sts, M1-R, k2; on left Front, k2, M1, knit to end. Purl 1 WS row.

Join Fronts

NEXT ROW (RS): Work across right Front sts, then left Front sts, breaking second ball of yarn. AT THE SAME TIME, when armholes measure same as for Back from marker to beginning of armhole shaping, shape armholes as for Back, ending with a WS row—96 (104, 112, 120, 128) sts when all shaping is complete.

BODY

Join Back and Front

NEXT ROW (RS): Work across Front sts, CO 0 (2, 4, 6, 8) sts for underarm, pm for left side and beginning of rnd, CO 0 (2, 4, 6, 8) sts, work across Back sts, CO 0 (2, 4, 6, 8) sts for underarm, pm for right side, CO 0 (2, 4, 6, 8) sts—192 (216, 240, 264, 288) sts. Join and, working in St st, work even for 2 (2¼, 2¼, 3, 3¼)".

Shape Waist

DECREASE RND: Decrease 4 sts this rnd, then every 8 rnds twice, as follows: [K2tog, knit to 2 sts before next marker, ssk, sm] twice—180 (204, 228, 252, 276) sts remain. Work even until piece measures 6 (6½, 6¾, 7, 7½)" from underarm. ✳ *Customizing Tip:* If you wish to convert this sweater into a dress, simply work the hip shaping as given, but delay beginning the stripe pattern until the piece measures approximately 13" from desired total length, so that the stripes appear on the skirt. Of course, you will need to purchase additional yarn if you work the sweater longer than shown. ✳

Cream-colored velvet elastic trim pairs beautifully with the vibrant colors in this sweater.

Shape Hips

NEXT RND: Change to A and work Rnds 1-92 of Body Stripe Pattern once. AT THE SAME TIME, when piece measures 9 ½ (9 ¾, 10 ¼, 10 ½, 11)", begin hip shaping as follows:

NEXT RND: [K30 (34, 38, 42, 46), pm] 6 times, omitting final pm.

INCREASE RND: Continuing in Body Stripe Pattern, increase 6 sts this rnd, then every 7 rnds 9 times, as follows: [Knit to marker, yo, sm] 6 times—240 (264, 288, 312, 336) sts. *Note: Work yos through the back loop on rnds following increase rnds.*

Work even until piece measures 19 ¼ (19 ½, 20, 20 ¼, 20 ½)" from armhole, changing to MC once Body Stripe Pattern is complete. BO all sts.

SLEEVES

With RS facing, using shorter circ needle and MC, and beginning at center of underarm, pick up and knit 66 (74, 82, 90, 98) sts evenly around armhole (see tutorial on page 22). Pm for beginning of rnd and join.

Shape Cap

ROW 1: K44 (49, 54, 60, 65), wrp-t.

ROW 2: P22 (24, 26, 30, 32), wrp-t.

ROWS 3-40 (42, 44, 46, 48): Work to wrapped st from row before previous row, hide wrap, wrp-t—3 (5, 7, 8, 10) sts remain unworked on either side of underarm marker.

Note: Change to dpns if necessary for number of sts on needle.

Work even until piece measures 13 (13 ¾, 14 ½, 15 ¼, 15 ¾)" from underarm, hiding remaining wrap as you come to it.

NEXT RND: K11 (13, 15, 15, 17), pm, [k11 (12, 13, 15, 16), pm] 4 times, knit to end.

Shape Cuff

INCREASE RND: Increase 6 sts this rnd, then every 8 rnds twice, as follows: [Knit to next marker, M1, sm] 6 times—84 (92, 100, 108, 116) sts.

NEXT RND: Change to A and work Rnds 1-25 of Sleeve Stripe Pattern once. Change to MC and work even until piece measures 20 ¾ (21 ½, 22 ¼, 23, 23 ½)" from underarm. BO all sts.

FINISHING

Work 4 rnds sc (see tutorial on page 150) along bottom edge. Work 1 rnd sc around neckline, working 1 sc in every st across Back neck and 1 sc in every other row at neck edges. Sew ribbon to WS of hem (see tutorial on page 149).

Sleeve Edging

With RS facing, using crochet hook and holding elastic cord parallel to edge, work 1 rnd sc around Sleeve edge and cord (see tutorial on page 155). Adjust elastic cord to desired measurements, tie in knot to secure, and weave ends into rnd of sc. Weave in all ends. Block as desired.

jill's dress

This dress pays homage to one of my favorite clothing designers, Jill Anderson, who often uses trim to detail the outside of her sewn dresses. In my knitted version, I mimicked this effect with lines of crochet. Although I chose to use the same color for the seams shown here, you could easily experiment with a contrasting color and make them even more pronounced.

BACK

Using waste yarn and provisional CO (see tutorial on page 16), CO 76 (80, 84, 88, 92, 96, 100) sts. Working in St st and beginning with a WS row, work 2 rows even.

NEXT ROW (WS): P12 (13, 14, 15, 16, 17, 18), place marker (pm), p52 (54, 56, 58, 60, 62, 64), pm, work to end.

Shape Shoulders

ROWS 1 (RS) AND 2: Work to second marker, slip marker (sm), work 3 (4, 4, 4, 5, 5, 5) sts, wrp-t (see tutorial on page 19).

ROWS 3 AND 4: Work to wrapped st from row before previous row, hide wrap, work 3 (3, 4, 4, 4, 5, 5) sts, wrp-t.

Work even, hiding remaining wraps as you come to them, until armholes measure 6¾" from end of shoulder shaping, ending with a WS row.

Shape Armholes

INCREASE ROW (RS): Increase 1 st each edge this row, then every other row 1 (3, 5, 7, 9, 11, 13) time(s), as follows: K2, M1-R, knit to last 2 sts, M1, k2—80 (88, 96, 104, 112, 120, 128) sts. Purl 1 WS row. Break yarn and transfer sts to waste yarn for Body.

sizes

2X-Small (X-Small, Small, Medium, Large, X-Large, 2X-Large)

finished measurements

32 (35¼, 38½, 41½, 44¾, 48, 51¼)" bust

yarn

Elsebeth Lavold Silky Tweed (40% silk/30% cotton/20% merino wool/10% viscose; 131 yards/50 grams): 10 (11, 12, 13, 14, 16, 17) hanks #11 Straw

needles

One 32" (80 cm) long circular (circ) needle size US 5 (3.75 mm)

Change needle size if necessary to obtain correct gauge.

notions

Waste yarn; stitch markers; stitch holders; crochet hook size US E/4 (3.5 mm)

gauge

20 sts and 30 rows = 4" (10 cm) in Stockinette stitch (St st)

FRONT

With RS facing, carefully unravel Provisional CO and place sts on circ needle for Front. Mark armhole edge for top of armhole.

NEXT ROW (RS): K12 (13, 14, 15, 16, 17, 18); join a second ball of yarn, BO 52 (54, 56, 58, 60, 62, 64) center neck sts, knit to end. Working BOTH SIDES AT THE SAME TIME using separate balls of yarn, working in St st, and beginning with a RS row, work 2 rows even. Shape shoulders as for Back, ending with a WS row.

Shape Neck

Note: Neck and armhole shaping will be worked at the same time; please read entire section through before beginning.

INCREASE ROW (RS): Increase 1 st each neck edge this row, then every other row 25 (26, 27, 28, 29, 30, 31) times, as follows: On right Front, knit to last 2 sts, M1-R, k2; on left Front, k2, M1, knit to end. Purl 1 WS row.

Join Fronts

NEXT ROW (RS): Work across right Front sts, then left Front sts, breaking second ball of yarn. AT THE SAME TIME, when armholes measure same as for Back from marker to beginning of armhole shaping, shape armholes as for Back, ending with a WS row—80 (88, 96, 104, 112, 120, 128) sts.

BODY

Join Back and Front

With RS facing, work across Front sts, pm, work across Back sts from waste yarn—160 (176, 192, 208, 224, 240, 256) sts. Pm for beginning of rnd and join. Work even until piece measures 14 (14 ¼, 14 ¾, 15, 15 ½, 15 ¾, 16 ¼)" from underarm.

Establish Center Front and Back

NEXT RND: K40 (44, 48, 52, 56, 60, 64), pm for center Front, knit to 40 (44, 48, 52, 56, 60, 64) past left side marker, pm for center Back, knit to end.

INCREASE RND: Increase 8 sts this rnd, then every 8 rnds 7 times, as follows: K2, M1, work to 1 st before center Front marker, M1, k1, sm, k1, M1, work to 2 sts before left side marker, M1, k2, sm, k2, M1, work to 1 st before center Back marker, M1, k1, sm, k1, M1, work to last 2 sts, M1, k2—224 (240, 256, 272, 288, 304, 320) sts. Work even until piece measures 26 ¼ (27, 27 ½, 28, 28 ¼, 28 ¾, 29 ¼)" from underarm. BO all sts loosely.

FINISHING

Work 1 rnd sc (see tutorial on page 150) around armholes and neckline, working 1 sc in every st across Back neck and 1 sc in every other row at neck edges and around armholes. Work crochet "seam" as shown in schematic (see tutorial on page 126). Weave in all ends. Block as desired.

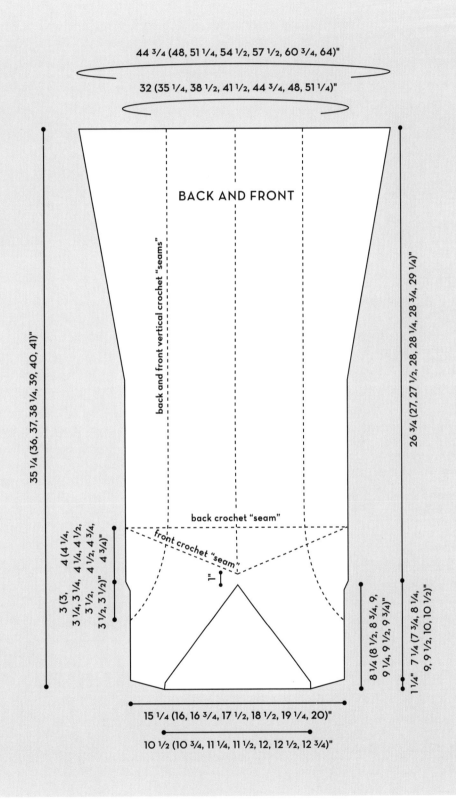

44 ³/₄ (48, 51 ¹/₄, 54 ¹/₂, 57 ¹/₂, 60 ³/₄, 64)"

32 (35 ¹/₄, 38 ¹/₂, 41 ¹/₂, 44 ³/₄, 48, 51 ¹/₄)"

BACK AND FRONT

back and front vertical crochet "seams"

26 ³/₄ (27, 27 ¹/₂, 28, 28 ¹/₄, 28 ³/₄, 29 ¹/₄)"

35 ¹/₄ (36, 37, 38 ¹/₄, 39, 40, 41)"

back crochet "seam"

front crochet "seam"

3 (3, 4 (4 ¹/₄, 3 ¹/₄, 3 ¹/₄, 4 ¹/₄, 4 ¹/₂, 3 ¹/₂, 4 ¹/₂, 4 ³/₄, 3 ¹/₂, 3 ¹/₂)" 4 ³/₄)"

1"

8 ¹/₄ (8 ¹/₂, 8 ³/₄, 9, 9 ¹/₄, 9 ¹/₂, 9 ³/₄)"

1 ¹/₄" 7 ¹/₄ (7 ³/₄, 8 ¹/₄, 9, 9 ¹/₂, 10, 10 ¹/₂)"

15 ¹/₄ (16, 16 ³/₄, 17 ¹/₂, 18 ¹/₂, 19 ¹/₄, 20)"

10 ¹/₂ (10 ³/₄, 11 ¹/₄, 11 ¹/₂, 12, 12 ¹/₂, 12 ³/₄)"

Vertical Crochet "Seam"

Begin by designating one vertical column of knit stitches for the "seam." Insert the crochet hook into the stitch (A), draw up a loop, and work sc in every other stitch along the column (B and C). To connect "seams" to outer rows of sc (as at the Back neck), draw the yarn through the final stitch of the finished "seam"; with a tapestry needle, secure the tail to the base of the outer row (C).

Horizontal and Diagonal Crochet "Seams"

Draw a piece of waste yarn through one side of every other stitch of the designated row (D) or diagonal (E). With your working yarn and crochet hook, work a row of sc along the waste yarn line, working into one side of the garment stitches and making sure to avoid catching the waste yarn (F and G). When the "seams" are finished, remove the waste yarn.

over-the-ocean slippers

From the age of ten onward, I was fortunate to be able to spend my summers in Austria with my mother's family. I would always bring a pair of Isotoner slippers with me for the long flight, finding it a treat to walk around the plane so informally. I designed these slippers hoping to capture some of the comfort of that original pair, but with an even homier touch since these are handmade. I crafted the soles using a hole punch and piece of leather, which provides some slip-resistant durability, and then gathered the top edges together with elastic cord—a quick, efficient shaping trick.

NOTE

✳ You may find it easier to use two circular needles for this project (see Special Techniques, page 157), rather than double-pointed needles (dpns). If your preference is for dpns but you find it a bit tight working the first few rounds, consider using 6 dpns, 3 along each side.

SOLE

Make a photocopy or scan of the Sole template, enlarging it 150% so that Sole measures 9 (9½, 10¼)" long from back of heel. Using template, cut out 2 pieces of leather, flipping template over for second Sole so as to have a right and left Sole. Mark 96 (112, 128) spaces approximately ¼" in from the edge and ³⁄₁₆" apart on each Sole. Punch a hole in each space using the smallest hole setting.

With RS of Sole facing, using crochet hook and 2 strands of yarn held together, and beginning at heel, work 1 sc (see tutorial on page 150) in each hole; slip st to first sc to join. Fasten off, but do not break yarn.

sizes
Small (Medium, Large)

finished measurements
9 (9½, 10¼)" long from back of heel

yarn
Sheldridge Soft Touch Heather (85% superwash wool/15% nylon; 185 yards/60 grams): 2 hanks Toasted Chestnut

needles
One or two 24" (60 cm) long or longer circular (circ) needles or one set of five (or more) double-pointed needles (dpn) size US 5 (3.75 mm), as preferred (see Note)

Change needle size if necessary to obtain correct gauge.

notions
Crochet hook size US E/4 (3.5 mm); stitch markers; 3 yards thin, round elastic cord; one 8½" x 11" piece leather or suede; leather hole punch

gauge
11 sts and 13 rnds = 2" (5 cm) in Stockinette stitch (St st), using 2 strands of yarn held together

Using same yarn, pick up and knit 1 st in each sc around Sole—96 (112, 128) sts. Place marker (pm) for beginning of rnd and join. Pm at toe, making sure you have same number of sts between markers on each side.

HEEL
Shape Heel

ROW 1 (RS): K7 (6, 7), wrp-t (see tutorial on page 19).

ROW 2: P14 (12, 14), wrp-t.

ROWS 3-6 (8, 8): Work to wrap from row before previous row, hide wrap, work 7 (6, 7) sts, wrp-t.

Knit 1 rnd, hiding remaining wrap as you come to it.

TOE
Shape Toe

ROW 1 (RS): Knit to 4 sts past toe marker, wrp-t.

ROW 2: P8, wrp-t.

ROWS 3-10 (12, 14): Work to wrap from row before previous row, hide wrap, work 3 sts, wrp-t.

ROWS 11 (13, 15) AND 12 (14, 16): Work to wrap from row before previous row, hide wrap, work 2 sts, wrp-t.

Knit 1 rnd, hiding remaining wrap as you come to it. BO all sts.

FINISHING
Using crochet hook and 2 strands of yarn held together, and holding elastic cord parallel to BO edge, work 1 rnd sc around BO edge and cord (see tutorial on page 155). Adjust elastic cord to desired measurements, tie in knot to secure, and weave ends into rnd of sc. With tapestry needle and 2 strands of yarn held together, work backstitch (see Special Techniques, page 157) in each hole along Sole. Weave in all ends.

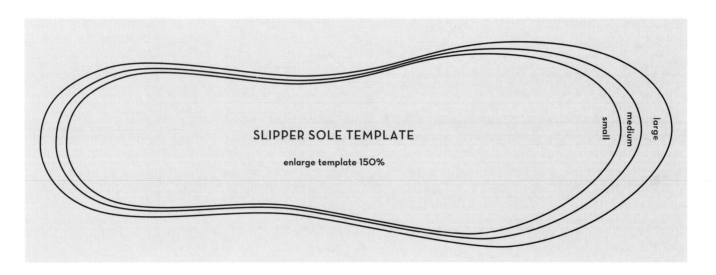

SLIPPER SOLE TEMPLATE

enlarge template 150%

small
medium
large

chrysler skirt

I never get tired of looking at the Chrysler Building and find the sight of its spire pure magic. This skirt mimics the building's chevron motif and the color of the sky on evenings I've enjoyed it most. The stitch pattern is somewhat open, which provides fun layering possibilities. We used a dark slip in the photo at left, but you could easily wear one in a brighter shade and have it peek through.

WAISTBAND

CO 138 (160, 184, 208) sts. Place marker (pm) for beginning of rnd and join, being careful not to twist sts. Work 10 rnds in Garter st (purl 1 rnd, knit 1 rnd), increase 18 (22, 24, 26) sts evenly on last rnd—156 (182, 208, 234) sts.

SKIRT

Work Rnds 1-6 of Chevron Ridge Pattern from Chart 6 (6, 6, 7) times, then Rnds 7-12 once, working increases as indicated in Chart—180 (210, 240, 270) sts.

Work Rnds 13-18 of Chart 5 (5, 5, 6) times; skirt measures approximately 12½ (12½, 12½, 14½)".

Shape Hip
NEXT RND: Work Rnds 19-24 of Chart once, working increases as indicated in Chart—204 (238, 272, 306) sts. Work Rnds 25-30 of Chart until piece measures 22 (23, 24, 25)" from the beginning, ending with Rnd 27 of Chart. Work 10 Rnds in Garter st, beginning with a purl rnd. BO all sts loosely.

FINISHING

With RS facing and holding elastic cord parallel to CO edge, work 1 rnd sc around Waistband and cord (see tutorial on page 155). Adjust elastic cord to desired measurement, tie in knot to secure, and weave ends into rnd of sc. Weave in all ends. Block as desired.

sizes
X-Small (Small, Medium, Large)

finished measurements
36 (42, 48, 54)" hip
23¼ (24¼, 25¼, 26¼)" long

yarn
Karabella Aurora 8 (100% extrafine merino wool; 98 yards/50 grams): 10 (12, 14, 16) balls #23 Blue

needles
One 29" (70 cm) long circular (circ) needle size US 7 (4.5 mm)

Change needle size if necessary to obtain correct gauge.

notions
Stitch markers; crochet hook size US G/6 (4 mm); 1 yard thin, round elastic cord

gauge
20 sts and 24 rnds = 4" (10 cm) in Chevron Ridge Pattern from Chart

CHEVRON RIDGE PATTERN

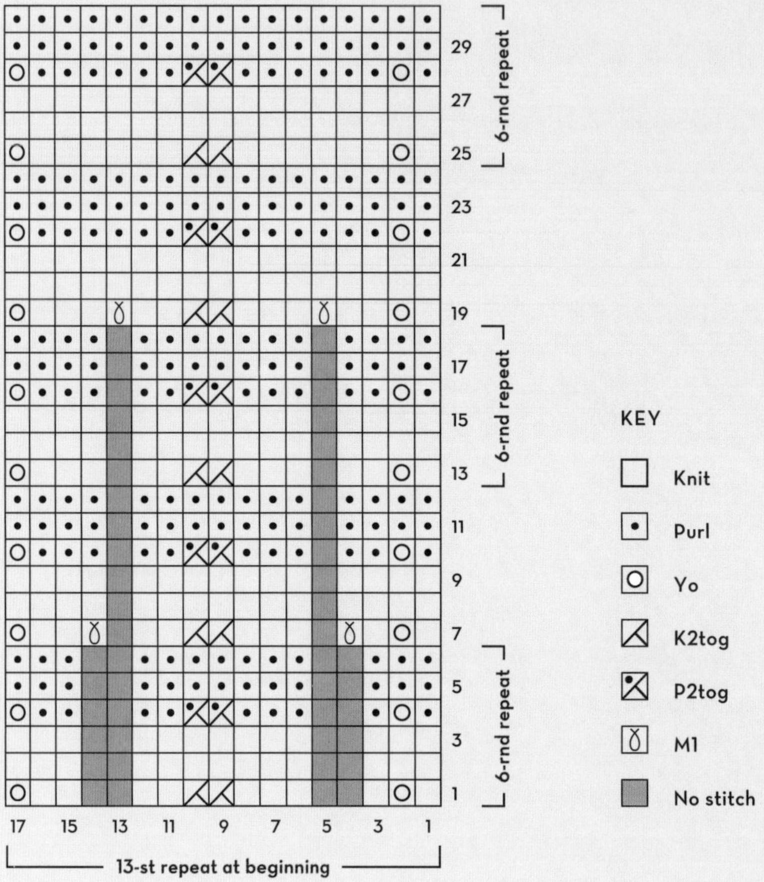

29
27
25
23
21
19
17
15
13
11
9
7
5
3
1
6-rnd repeat
6-rnd repeat
6-rnd repeat
17
15
13
11
9
7
5
3
1
13-st repeat at beginning
KEY
Knit
Purl
Yo
K2tog
P2tog
M1
No stitch

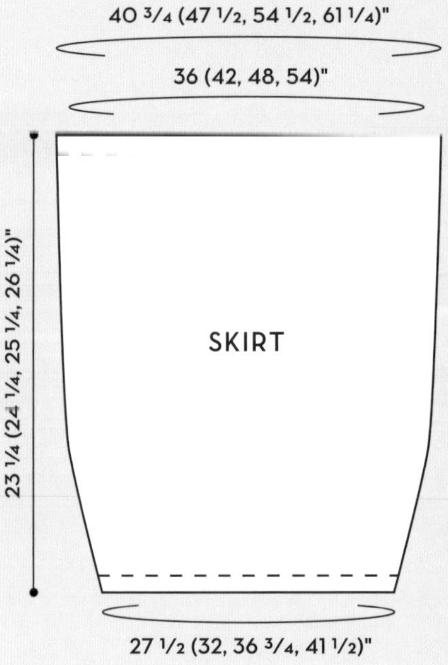

40 3/4 (47 1/2, 54 1/2, 61 1/4)"
36 (42, 48, 54)"
23 1/4 (24 1/4, 25 1/4, 26 1/4)"
SKIRT
27 1/2 (32, 36 3/4, 41 1/2)"

knitted jewelry

When Barbara Walker told me that she once used fishing line to craft durable bags for clothespins it made me wonder about other unconventional materials that could be knitted. I've experimented with quite a few things since then—twine, fine leather strips, and even VCR tape—but so far, my best find has been a flexible 24-karat gold and sterling silver wire from my local beading store. Unlike regular wire, it's coated with nylon, which makes it especially flexible and easy to knit.

BEADS FOR BRACELET (make 8)

CO 25 sts. Work in St st for 4 rows, slipping the first st of every row. BO all sts, leaving an 8" tail. Weave in CO tail using tapestry needle. With WS facing and beginning with narrow end, roll tightly to form a round bead. Secure using remaining wire tail, then weave in end.

Finishing

Cut a 12" piece of wire. String crimp bead onto wire, then loop half of toggle clasp set before threading it through crimp bead once more. Use pliers to set crimp bead in place. String beads onto wire, alternating with glass beads. Use remaining crimp bead to attach second half of toggle clasp to other end.

RING

CO 4 (8) sts. Work in Garter st (knit every row) for 2¾" or until piece fits comfortably around finger. Cut wire, leaving a 9" tail. BO all sts using sewn BO, as follows: Thread tail through tapestry needle. Working from right to left, *thread tapestry needle through first 2 sts purlwise, then through front of first st knitwise. Pull wire snug and slip st off needle. Repeat from * until all sts are BO.

Finishing

Sew CO edge to BO edge. Weave in all ends.

finished measurements

BRACELET: 8½" long

RINGS: Approximately ½ (1)" wide

materials

BRACELET: Extreme Flex wire by Soft Flex Company (.024 diameter/30 feet): 2 rolls #EXT0243OGLD 24K gold

RINGS: Extreme Flex wire by Soft Flex Company (.024 diameter/30 feet): 1 roll #EXT0243OGLD 24K gold or #EXT0243OSLV sterling silver

needles

BRACELET: One pair straight needles size US 3 (3.25 mm)

RINGS: One pair straight needles size US 0 (2 mm)

Change needle size if necessary to obtain correct gauge.

notions

BRACELET: Tapestry needle; eight ½"-round glass beads; 1 toggle clasp set; two 2x2 mm crimp beads; long-nose pliers

RINGS: Tapestry needle

gauge

BRACELET: 7 sts and 8 rows = 1" (2.5 cm) in Stockinette stitch (St st)

RINGS: 8 sts and 16 rows = 1" (2.5 cm) in Garter stitch (knit every row)

promenade dress

The easy-yet-tailored look of this dress is a nod to the relaxed mornings I spent at the Brooklyn Heights promenade when I first moved to New York. For this dress, I focused on subtle details, including vertical lines of crochet at the bodice and a sturdy single-crochet button band.

NOTE

✳ After the initial Provisional CO, use Backward Loop CO for any other COs in this pattern (see Special Techniques, page 157).

BACK

Using circ needle, waste yarn, and Provisional CO (see tutorial on page 16), CO 86 (90, 94, 98, 102) sts. Working in St st and beginning with a knit row, work 1 row even.

NEXT ROW (WS): P23 (24, 26, 27, 28), place marker (pm), p40 (42, 42, 44, 46), pm, purl to end.

Shape Shoulders

ROWS 1 (RS) AND 2: Work to second marker, slip marker (sm), work 3 (3, 4, 3, 3) sts, wrp-t (see tutorial on page 19).

ROWS 3–10: Work to wrapped st from row before previous row, hide wrap, work 3 (3, 3, 4, 4) sts, wrp-t.

Work even in St st, hiding remaining wraps as you come to them, until armholes measure 5¾ (5¼, 5¼, 5 ¼, 6)" from end of shoulder shaping, ending with a WS row.

Shape Armholes

INCREASE ROW (RS): Increase 1 st each side this row, then every other row 3 (7, 7, 9, 11) times, as follows: K2, M1-R, knit to last 2 sts, M1, k2—94 (106, 110, 118, 126) sts. Break yarn and transfer sts to waste yarn for Back.

sizes
X-Small (Small, Medium, Large, X-Large)

finished measurements
31¼ (35¼, 39¼, 43¼, 47¼)" bust

yarn
Louet Gems Sport Weight (100% merino wool; 225 yards/100 grams): 8 (9, 10, 11, 13) hanks #49 Charcoal

needles
One 32" (80 cm) long circular (circ) needle size US 5 (3.75 mm)

One set of five double-pointed needles (dpn) size US 5 (3.75 mm)

Change needle size if necessary to obtain correct gauge.

notions
Waste yarn; stitch markers; crochet hook size US F/5 (3.75 mm); sewing needle and matching thread; 5 (5, 6, 6, 6) ½" buttons; two ¼"-wide snaps

gauge
24 sts and 32 rows = 4" (10 cm) in Stockinette stitch (St st)

FRONTS

With RS facing, carefully unravel Provisional CO and place sts on circ needle for Front. Mark armhole edge for top of armhole.

NEXT ROW (RS): K23 (24, 26, 27, 28); join a second ball of yarn, BO 40 (42, 42, 44, 46) sts, knit to end. Working BOTH SIDES AT THE SAME TIME using separate balls of yarn, work 2 rows in St st. Shape shoulders as for Back.

Work even, hiding remaining wraps as you come to them, until neck edge measures 2", ending with a WS row.

Shape Neck

INCREASE ROW (RS): Increase 1 st each side this row, then every row 10 (11, 11, 12, 13) times, as follows: On right Front, knit to last 2 sts, M1-R, k2; on left Front, k2, M1, knit to end—34 (36, 38, 40, 42) sts each side. Work 1 WS row even.

NEXT ROW (RS): CO 6 sts at each neck edge once—40 (42, 44, 46, 48) sts each side.

Work even until armholes measure same as for Back from marker to beginning of armhole shaping. Shape armholes as for Back, ending with a RS row—44 (50, 52, 56, 60) sts each side. Break yarn for left Front.

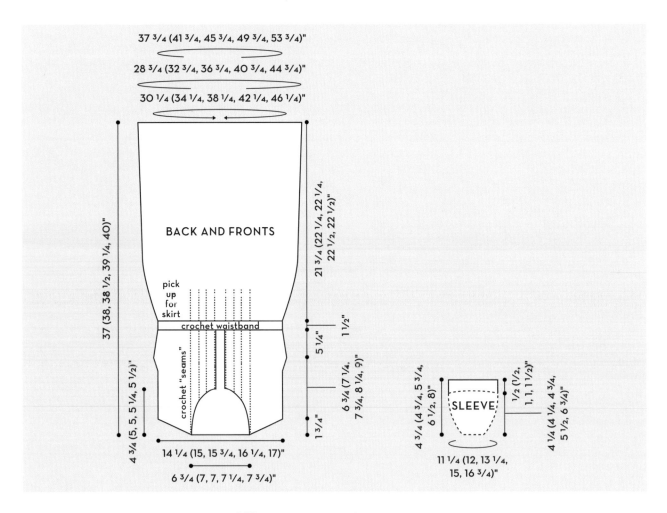

37 3/4 (41 3/4, 45 3/4, 49 3/4, 53 3/4)"

28 3/4 (32 3/4, 36 3/4, 40 3/4, 44 3/4)"

30 1/4 (34 1/4, 38 1/4, 42 1/4, 46 1/4)"

BACK AND FRONTS

37 (38, 38 1/2, 39 1/4, 40)"

21 3/4 (22 1/4, 22 1/4, 22 1/2, 22 1/2)"

pick up for skirt

crochet waistband

crochet "seams"

1 1/2"

5 1/4"

6 3/4 (7 1/4, 7 3/4, 8 1/4, 9)"

1 3/4"

4 3/4 (5, 5, 5 1/4, 5 1/2)"

14 1/4 (15, 15 3/4, 16 1/4, 17)"

6 3/4 (7, 7, 7 1/4, 7 3/4)"

SLEEVE

4 3/4 (4 3/4, 5 3/4, 6 1/2, 8)"

1/2 (1/2, 1, 1, 1 1/2)"

4 1/4 (4 1/4, 4 3/4, 5 1/2, 6 3/4)"

11 1/4 (12, 13 1/4, 15, 16 3/4)"

BODY

Join Back and Fronts

With WS facing, transfer Back, then left Front sts to left-hand end of circ needle. Your sts should now be in the following order, from right to left, with WS facing: right Front, Back, left Front. Using yarn attached to right Front, purl across right Front sts, CO 0 (0, 8, 12, 16) sts for underarm, purl across Back sts, CO 0 (0, 8, 12, 16) sts for underarm, purl across left Front sts—182 (206, 230, 254, 278) sts. Do not join. Working back and forth, work even until piece measures 3" from underarm, ending with a WS row.

Shape Body

DECREASE ROW 1 (RS): K3, [k20 (23, 26, 29, 32), k2tog] 8 times, k3—174 (198, 222, 246, 270) sts remain. Work 7 rows even.

DECREASE ROW 2 (RS): K3, [k19 (22, 25, 28, 31), k2tog] 8 times, k3—166 (190, 214, 238, 262) sts remain. Work 8 rows even. Piece measures 5¼" from underarm. ✳ *Customizing Tip:* You may wish to transfer your stitches to waste yarn and try the piece on at this point, before binding off. The piece should sit comfortably below your bustline. Work additional rows if necessary to ensure proper fit. ✳ BO all sts.

Waistband

With RS facing, using crochet hook, work 1 sc in each BO st of Body (see tutorial on page 150). Work 4 rows sc. Fasten off.

Button Band

With RS facing, using crochet hook and beginning at neck edge, work 54 (54, 56, 58, 60) sc along left Front edge. Work 6 rows sc. Fasten off.

Buttonhole Band

With RS facing, using crochet hook and beginning at bottom edge, work 54 (54, 56, 58, 60) sc along right Front edge.

NEXT ROW: Ch 1 to turn (counts as first st), sc in each sc to end. Repeat last row once.

BUTTONHOLE ROW: Ch 1 to turn, 5 (5, 1, 2, 3) sc, [skip 2, ch 2, 8 sc] 4 (4, 5, 5, 5) times, skip 2, ch 2, 6 (6, 2, 3, 4) sc.

NEXT ROW: Ch 1 to turn, sc in each sc to end, working 2 sc into each ch 2 space. Work 2 rows sc. Fasten off.

SKIRT

Arrange Bands so that Buttonhole Band overlaps Button Band and garment is RS out. Using circ needle, pick up and knit 6 sts, working through BOTH LAYERS of Bands to join them; picking up 1 st in each sc, pick up and knit 40 (46, 52, 58, 64) sts along Waistband, pm for left side and beginning of rnd, pick up and knit 86 (98, 110, 122, 134) sts, pm for right side, pick up and knit 40 (46, 52, 58, 64) sts to Button Band, join and work to beginning of rnd—172 (196, 220, 244, 268) sts. Work even in St st until piece measures 5" from Waistband.

Shape Skirt

INCREASE RND 1: *M1, k43 (49, 55, 61, 67); repeat from * around—176 (200, 224, 248, 272) sts. Work 8 rnds even.

NEXT RND: *K17 (20, 20, 23, 26), pm, [k18 (20, 24, 26, 28), pm] 3 times, knit to marker; repeat from * once.

INCREASE RND 2: Increase 10 sts this rnd, then every 9 rnds 4 times, as follows: Knit to marker, M1; repeat from * to end—226 (250, 274, 298, 322) sts. Work even until piece measures 21¾ (22¼, 22¼, 22½, 22½)" from pick-up rnd. BO all sts.

SLEEVES

With RS facing, beginning at center of underarm, pick up and knit 68 (72, 80, 90, 100) sts evenly around armhole (see tutorial on page 22). Pm for beginning of rnd and join.

Shape Cap

ROW 1 (RS): K46 (48, 52, 57, 64), wrp-t.

ROW 2: P24 (24, 24, 24, 28), wrp-t.

ROWS 3-34 (34, 38, 44, 52): Work to wrapped st from row before previous row, hide wrap, wrp-t—6 (8, 10, 12, 11) sts remain unworked on either side of underarm marker.

Note: Change to dpns when necessary for number of sts on needle.

Work even until piece measures ½ (½, 1, 1, 1½)" or to desired length from underarm, hiding remaining wrap as you come to it. BO all sts.

FINISHING

Using crochet hook, work 2 rnds sc along Sleeve openings and 4 rnds along bottom edge.

Collar

With RS facing, using crochet hook and beginning at right Front neck edge, work 34 (35, 35, 37, 38) sc along right Front neck edge (including top of Buttonhole Band), 40 (42, 42, 44, 46) sc along Back neck, and 34 (35, 35, 37, 38) sc along left Front neck edge (including top of Button Band)—108 (112, 112, 118, 122) sts. Work 4 rows sc. Fasten off.

Work crochet "seam" detail as follows (see tutorial on page 126): Beginning at right neck edge in first column of sts directly next to buttonhole band, work crochet "seam" detail to Waistband; repeat every 6th column of sts 3 times, moving toward the right armhole, each time working from neck edge to Waistband. Work additional crochet "seam" details below Waistband for 3½", aligning each with "seam" detail above. Repeat for left side of Dress, working a mirror image of right Front to match. Sew buttons opposite buttonholes. Sew snaps to collar, sewing female sides to top RS edge of Button Band and male sides to top WS edge of Buttonhole Band, spaced approximately ½" apart. Weave in all ends. Block as desired.

finishing

When many knitters hear the word *finishing*, they think of sewing seams together and weaving in ends. And although there is no reprieve as of yet for having to weave in ends, one of the benefits of Barbara Walker's seamless top-down method used for the projects in this book is that it largely eliminates the need to sew seams. Instead, you can use your time to sew beautiful silk, velvet, or lace trim onto the inside edges of your necklines and hems, crochet borders to keep edges straight and clean, and crochet elastic cord into your garments (such as at the waist or sleeves) as a shaping tool. Following is an overview of all of these simple techniques and how I use them in the projects in this book. All of these techniques help to give knitted garments a beautiful, couture-like finish.

TRIM

"Things should always look as good on the inside as they do on the outside," dressmaker Jill Anderson explained as I stood in her shop in New York's East Village, examining the inside of one of her dresses. It was the first time I had seen trim used to enclose the seam allowance on the inside of a sewn item, and I was very impressed with how well-crafted it made the dress feel. Inspired, I began to experiment with trim on my knitted items and soon discovered that it produced beautiful results. On a practical level, trim adds structure and prevents edges from curling. On an aesthetic level, it refines the garment.

From top: Sheer trim on the Soho Smocked Dress (page 29); seam binding on the Feather Dress (page 99); velvet trim on the Museum Tunic (page 91); lace trim on the Suspension Dress (page 57).

Selecting Trim

I've listed some of my favorite trims here, but I encourage you to explore your local sewing shops and trim stores and to experiment with any type of trim that catches your eye. As a general rule, choose trim that can stretch when lining the inside edge of a sleeve or neck opening; if you use a non-stretch trim, you may not be able to get your head or arms through the openings. For edges that are open and don't necessarily need to maintain elasticity, such as the bottom inside edge of a cardigan or coat, this is, of course, less important. The width of trim you select is entirely a matter of personal preference.

Elastic trim (A): The matte side of elastic trim is especially lovely and is a perfect border for any item that needs a bit of extra give (such as a hat or neck opening). I usually choose ½"-wide elastic because the crocheted edges upon which I typically sew it are that width, but for most projects, any width you choose will work. For the Mulberry Hat on page 87, sewing a band of elastic to the outside helped shape the hat, and provided a practical design element.

Seam binding (B): This is one of my favorite trims to use because it is available in an astounding range of colors and it is usually very inexpensive, making it possible to gather a whole palette with which to experiment. I chose a rich olive color for the edges of the Wrap-It-Up Dress on page 69 and the thin, delicate binding helped add a bit of color to the skirt opening, which can sometimes flip back when you walk.

Sheer trim (C): The subtlest of all the choices, sheer trim adds a hint of color that, when paired with yarn, can be stunning. Most sheer trim has a fine edge in a darker color, and when you use thread in that color to sew it on, the stitches become practically invisible. I used sheer trim along the inside bottom edge of the Blueberry Cardigan on page 111.

Lace trim (D): I prefer to use lace in the same color as my yarn, but you can easily choose a shade lighter or darker or a different color for contrast. There is something very special about trimming your knits with lace and simply having the pleasure of knowing that it is there. For knitted dresses especially, like the Suspension Dress on page 57, lace instantly refines the look. Cotton lace is a rugged, sturdy option, and stretch varieties also work quite well.

Stretch velvet (E): The softness and rich, saturated color of velvet trim always looks beautiful against a backdrop of knitted stitches. I used a thin version to trim the edges of the Accordion Cowl on page 75 and the Keffiyeh Wrap on page 81, and a more substantial width for the Museum Tunic on page 91 and the Coney Sweater on page 117. Sewn stitches disappear into velvet with ease, making it an especially great trim to use if you're new to hand-sewing.

Sewing Trim onto Knits

No elaborate sewing skills are required here. For a clean and polished result, I just make sure that my trim and thread match well. All of the trims mentioned above can be sewn on by hand using a medium-length sharp sewing needle, thread, and slip stitches, as follows:

1: To start, cut your trim to the length of the area to be covered. Thread a needle with a single ply of thread and secure the end with a knot. Come up through the back of your trim and pull the needle through to the front.

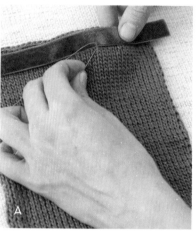

2: Bring the needle down just outside the edge of the trim and take a small stitch through the knit. Bring the needle up through the trim again, just to the right of the first stitch (**A**). Repeat until the entire edge of the trim along one side is stitched to the knitted item.

3: Repeat steps 1 and 2 to secure the other edge of the trim to the knitted item.

4: If working circularly, fold one end of the trim over ¼" at its edge, and lay it on top of the other end of the trim. Secure the ends neatly with a few slip stitches (**B**). If you are not sewing trim circularly, fold both ends of the trim over ¼" at the edges of the knitted border and sew in place with a few slip stitches.

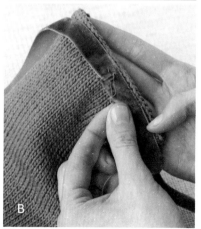

CROCHET

I use crocheted edges on almost all of my knitted designs because it provides a sturdy, non-curling edge (which I prefer to non-curling knit stitches like ribbing). A crocheted edge also provides an excellent, dense background upon which to apply trim. I use only two basic crochet stitches in the projects in this book—single crochet and double crochet.

Single Crochet

To work single crochet (sc) along the cast-on or bound-off edge of a knitted garment, insert the hook into the first stitch in the row (**A**). Insert the hook into the next stitch, yarn over the hook (**B**) and draw the yarn through the stitch (you now have two loops on your hook). Yarn over the hook again and draw the yarn through both loops on the hook. You now have one loop on your hook and have completed one single crochet (**C**). Repeat the steps shown in B and C in every knit stitch along the row until you have worked single crochet across the entire edge of the garment (**D**).

SINGLE CROCHET

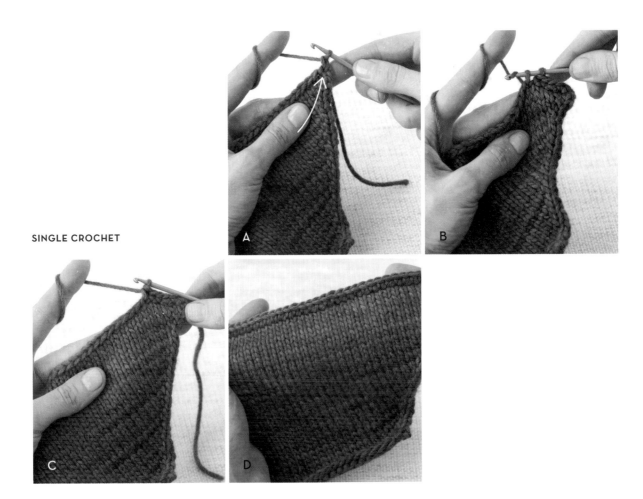

If you are working only one row of single crochet, snip the yarn at the end of the row (leaving a 6" tail). Pull the end of the yarn through the last loop on your hook and weave the end through your work. If you are working another row of single crochet, yarn over the hook at the end of the first row, draw a loop through the remaining loop on your hook, turn your work and insert the hook under both loops of the first stitch (the last single crochet stitch you worked in the previous row), and work single crochet into each stitch across the row to the end.

When working single crochet around a neckline, the sides of the neckline are worked along the edges of knitted rows. Work one single crochet in every other row (or every two rows out of three). If you work a single crochet in every row, the stitches around the neckline will be too crowded and will bunch up. When working across the cast-on or bound-off edge at the back neck, work single crochet in every stitch, as you would along the hem of a garment.

If you are working single crochet in the round, connect the first and last single crochet stitch by slipping your hook into the top of the first stitch worked; yarn over and pull a loop through the stitch and the loop on your hook to connect the stitches. Snip the yarn (leaving a 6" tail), pull the end of the yarn through the loop on your hook, and weave the end through your work.

Two rows of single crochet are worked along the back opening of the Subway Hat (page 39), then along its front edge, providing crisp edges and a perfect base upon which to sew the fleece lining.

Double Crochet

To work double crochet (dc) along the cast-on or bound-off edge of a knitted garment, insert the hook into the first stitch in the row, yarn over the hook, pull the loop through the stitch (this is a "chain one"); repeat twice to chain three stitches (this counts as the first double crochet of the row). Yarn over the hook again and insert the hook into the next knitted stitch (**A**); pull a loop up through the knitted stitch. You now have 3 stitches on your hook (**B**). Yarn over the hook and draw a loop through the first two stitches on the hook (you now have two loops on the hook) (**C**). Yarn over the hook again (**D**) and draw it through the remaining two loops on the hook (one loop remains on the hook) (**E**). You have now completed one double crochet stitch. Repeat steps shown in A through E in every stitch until you have reached the end of the row.

DOUBLE CROCHET

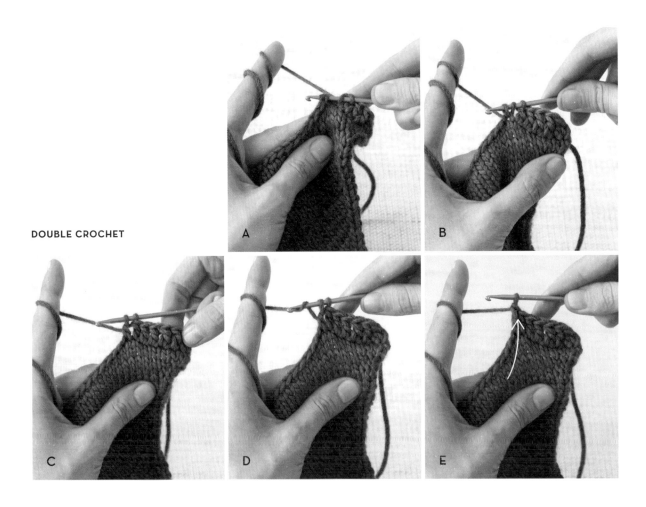

If you are working only one row of double crochet, snip the yarn at the end of the row (leaving a 6" tail); pull the end of the yarn through the last loop on your hook and weave the end through your work. If you are working another row of double crochet, chain 3, turn your work, yarn over the hook and insert the hook into the first stitch (the last double crochet stitch you worked in the previous row); work a double crochet into that stitch and each stitch across the row to the end.

If working in the round, connect the first and last double crochet stitch by slipping your hook into the top of the first stitch; yarn over and pull a loop through the stitch and the loop on your hook to connect the stitches. Snip the yarn (leaving a 6" tail), pull the end of the yarn through the loop on your hook, and weave the end through your work.

The double crochet at the sleeve cuffs and hem on the Feather Dress (page 99) provides a sturdy, attractive edge.

ELASTIC CORD

When I met with Barbara Walker, she showed me how she had woven thin black elastic cord inside the waistband edge of a skirt she had knit, and I was impressed with the smooth silhouette it provided. I decided to experiment with elastic as a shaping tool in my own knitting, and found that I could cleanly hide the elastic altogether by crocheting it into the edges of my pieces. When you crochet elastic to the edge of a knitted garment, it creates a tunnel for the elastic to move through, and smoothly cinches the fabric without pulling or bunching it. I liked this technique so much as a shaping tool that you'll find it in quite a few of the projects in this book, such as the Layered Ruffle Sweater (page 51), the Feather Dress (page 99), the Coney Sweater (page 117), the Seaport Skirt (page 65), and the Chrysler Skirt (page 133).

Elastic cord is crocheted into the front panels of the Layered Ruffle Sweater (page 51) to create its flounces.

Selecting Elastic Cord

Elastic cord can be found at most sewing supply stores, and is typically available in either black or white. I use white cord if I'm working with lighter yarn, and black cord for darker yarn. Elastic is most commonly sold in packets of about four yards, but if you use it often, I recommend purchasing a spool. The cord should be rounded and the width should be relatively thin. The thicker the cord, the bigger the knot you need to make to attach the two ends, and a big knot can be tricky to conceal. I usually work with 1/16" cord, though 3/32" and 1/8" also work well.

Attaching Elastic Cord

Lay the elastic cord along the edge of your garment (**A**) and with a crochet hook, enclose it in a border of single crochet (**B**). Pull the ends of the elastic to gather the stitches slightly. Tie the ends of the elastic cord in a tight knot and weave in the ends, tucking them into the row of single crochet to conceal. Sometimes I will use a tapestry needle to sew a few stitches around the spot where the knot is to help hide it further.

ATTACHING ELASTIC CORD

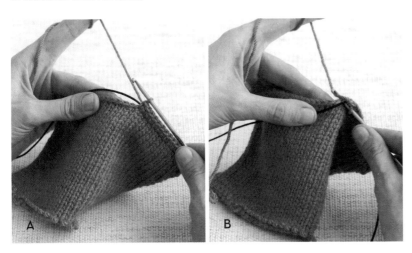

abbreviations

BO   Bind off

Ch   Chain

Circ   Circular

CO   Cast on

Dc   Double crochet

Dpn(s)   Double-pointed needle(s)

K   Knit

K1-f/b   Knit into the front loop and back loop of same stitch to increase one stitch.

K1-tbl   Knit one stitch through the back loop.

K2tog   Knit two stitches together.

M1 (make 1)   With the tip of the left-hand needle inserted from front to back, lift the strand between the two needles onto the left-needle; knit the strand through the back loop to increase one stitch.

M1-p (make 1 purlwise)   With the tip of the left-hand needle inserted from back to front, lift the strand between the two needles onto the left-hand needle; purl the strand through the front loop to increase one stitch.

M1-R (make 1-right slanting)   With the tip of the left-hand needle inserted from back to front, lift the strand between the two needles onto the left-hand needle; knit it through the front loop to increase one stitch.

P   Purl

Pm   Place marker

Psso (pass slipped stitch over)   Pass slipped stitch on right-hand needle over the stitches indicated in the instructions, as in binding off.

Rnd   Round

RS   Right side

Sc   Single crochet

Sm   Slip marker

Ssk (slip, slip, knit)   Slip next two stitches to right-hand needle one at a time as if to knit; return them to left-hand needle one at a time in their new orientation; knit them together through the back loops.

St(s)   Stitch(es)

Tbl   Through the back loop

Tog   Together

Wrp-t   Wrap and turn (see Short Rows tutorial on page 19)

WS   Wrong side

Wyib   With yarn in back

Wyif   With yarn in front

Yo   Yarnover

special techniques

Attaching Elastic Cord
See page 155

Backstitch
Bring tapestry needle up from WS to RS through first hole (A), then take needle back to WS through next hole (B). Bring yarn back to RS through third hole (C), then back to WS through B. Continue in this manner, working from WS to RS in empty hole beyond last hole worked, then going backwards one hole to go from RS to WS.

Backward Loop CO
Make a loop (using a slip knot) with the working yarn and place it on the right-hand needle [first stitch CO], *wind yarn around thumb clockwise, insert right-hand needle into the front of the loop on thumb, remove thumb and tighten stitch on needle; repeat from * for remaining stitches to be CO, or for casting on at the end of a row in progress.

Crocheted "Seams"
See page 126

Double Crochet (dc)
See page 152

Provisional CO
See page 16

Reading Charts
Unless otherwise specified in the instructions, when working straight, charts are read from right to left for RS rows, from left to right for WS rows. Row numbers are written at the beginning of each row. Numbers on the right indicate RS rows; numbers on the left indicate WS rows. When working circular, all rounds are read from right to left.

Short Rows
See page 19

Single Crochet (sc)
See page 150

Slip Stitch (Crochet)
Insert the crochet hook into the stitch to be worked, wrap the yarn over the hook, then pull the hook through the stitch just worked and the loop on the needle. Continue in this manner for the edge to be worked with slip stitch.

Working in the Round on Two Circular Needles
Using two circular needles of the same size, place half of your cast-on stitches on one needle and half on the other. Hold both ends of one needle in your hands; this is the working needle. Ignore the other needle and its stitches and let it hang out of your way. Knit across the stitches on the working needle. When you reach the end of these stitches, drop the first needle and pick up the other needle (this will now become the working needle) and work these stitches. Continue to work the needles alternately, taking care to maintain proper stitch tension between the needle joins to avoid loose stitches or a "ladder" effect.

Yarnover (yo)
Bring yarn forward (to the purl position), then place it in position to work the next stitch. If next st is to be knit, bring yarn over the needle and knit; if next stitch is to be purled, bring yarn over the needle and then forward again to the purl position and purl. Work the yarnover in pattern on the next row unless instructed otherwise.

sources

YARN

Be Sweet
1315 Bridgeway
Sausalito, CA 94965
www.besweetproducts.com

Blue Sky Alpacas, Inc.
P.O. Box 88
Cedar, MN 55011
www.blueskyalpacas.com

Debbie Bliss and Elsebeth Lavold
(distributed by Knitting Fever Inc.)
315 Bayview Avenue
Amityville, NY 11701
www.knittingfever.com

Karabella Yarns, Inc.
1201 Broadway
New York, NY 10001
www.karabellayarns.com

Louet North America
3425 Hands Road
Prescott, ON, Canada K0E 1T0
www.louet.com

Misti International, Inc.
P.O. Box 2532
Glen Ellyn, IL 60138
www.mistialpaca.com

Morehouse Merino
141 Milan Hill Road
Red Hook, NY 12571
www.morehousefarm.com

Shelridge Farm
c/o Buffy Taylor
P. O. Box 1345
Durham, ON, Canada N0G 1R0
www.shelridge.com

Tahki/Stacy Charles, Inc.
(Tahki Yarns and Filatura di Crosa)
70-30 80th Street, Building 36
Ridgewood, NY 11385
www.tahkistacycharles.com

TRIM

3G Trimming Corporation
230 West 38th Street, 1st Floor
New York, NY 10018
www.3gtrimming.com

C & C Button
230 West 38th Street
New York, NY 10018
(212) 944-7331

Daytona Braids & Trimmings
251 West 39th Street
New York, NY 10018
www.daytonatrim.com

Pacific Trimming, Inc.
218 West 38th Street
New York, NY 10018
www.pacifictrimming.com

Soft Flex Company
(for beading wire)
P.O. Box 80
Sonoma, CA 95476
www.softflexcompany.com

The Snap Source
P.O. Box 99733
Troy, MI 48099
www.snapsource.com

Steinlauf and Stoller
239 West 39th Street
New York, NY 10018
www.steinlaufandstoller.com

recommended reading

BOOKS

A Treasury of
Knitting Patterns

A Second Treasury of
Knitting Patterns

Charted Knitting Designs:
A Third Treasury of
Knitting Patterns

A Fourth Treasury of
Knitting Patterns
Barbara G. Walker
(Schoolhouse Press)
These four encyclopedic stitch
dictionaries are a wonderful
resource for anyone wanting to
design their own garments. The
third volume includes my favorite
stitch pattern: The Spider Panel.

Knitting from the Top
Barbara G. Walker
(Schoolhouse Press)
This book provides a compre-
hensive overview of all top-down
knitting techniques and forever
changed how I think about knitting
construction and design. I used it
to create almost all of the items in
this collection.

Knitting Without Tears
Elizabeth Zimmermann
(Scribners)
A staple in any knitter's library,
this book is packed with useful,
innovative, and easy-to-understand
knitting techniques and ideas.

ONLINE RESOURCES AND DVDs

www.knittinghelp.com
www.anniesattic.com
Both of these sites provide helpful
step-by-step tutorials and videos
for those who would like extra help
with basic knitting and crochet
techniques.

A Knitting Glossary (DVD)
with Elizabeth Zimmermann
and Meg Swansen
(Schoolhouse Press)
An infinitely useful collection of
knitting techniques and a rare
and delightful opportunity to
see Elizabeth Zimmermann and
her daughter Meg Swansen
demonstrate them.

acknowledgments

I would like to thank my mother, father, and sister for their constant support, encouragement, and love throughout the making of this book. Thank you to my first knitting mentors—Christine Auer, Maria Dominek, and Josefa Kritz—who bought me my first yarn and needles. This book also honors the memory of my grandmother, Julia Röessler, and aunt, Margit Mavromatis. I would like to thank three teachers who taught me to always remain curious and hopeful: Madeline Kelly, Beth Caufield, and Dydia DeLyser. Special thanks to Barbara Walker for writing *Knitting from the Top*, a book that has given me great joy and helped me to write this one. Thank you to gifted dressmaker Jill Anderson from whom I have learned so much. Thank you to Suss Cousins for believing in me and opening my eyes to a whole new world of knitting. Thank you to my dear and supportive friends: Lynn Buckley, Cecily Parks, Susan Ervolina, Jill Draper, Jonathan Lippincott, Michele Henjum, Heather Janbay, Jean Guirguis, Geni Haikin, Annie Wedekind, Thomas LeBien, Sarah Almond, and Leslie Scanlon. Thank you to my editor Melanie Falick, who from day one lifted me up and made me feel good about my work, and continued to encourage me when I was tired and unsure. Thank you to editor Liana Allday, who shepherded the entire project with great skill, patience, and grace. Thank you to Meg Swansen for her support at the outset of this project and throughout. Thank you to master knitter Amy Detjen, who always answered my questions with humor and kindness. Thank you to gifted technical editors Sue McCain and Véronik Avery. And thank you to Anna Christian for her beautiful graphic design. Finally, thank you to hard-working and talented photographer Gudrun Georges, her assistant Dirk Eusterbrock, and makeup artist Nickee David.

about the author

Kristina McGowan is a New York City-based knitwear designer. She holds a doctorate degree in social science from Syracuse University.